꿈꾸는 별
내 삶 백지로부터 하늘 끝까지

Dreaming star
My life from blank sheet to the end of the sky

김병임 지음

- Written by byungilm Kim(marian) -

마그마숲

프롤로그

　모든 것은 작은 한 점으로부터 시작되었다.
　생명이 작은 씨앗에서부터 시작되듯, '김영옥의 만다라'를 알게 된 것은 나에게 큰 행운이었다. 작은 내적인 움직임에서 처음 그려지는 나의 무의식의 마음이 점으로 표현되고 그 점이 모여서 선이 되고 면이 되고 더 커다란 원이 되고 집을 이루어 만다라를 만들었다. 나도 모르는 무의식의 세계들이 길을 내고 공간을 내고 마음의 응어리들이 몽이로 나타나게 되었다. 작업을 하면서 울기도 하고 많이 웃기도 하였다. 그리고 헤르만 헷세의 소설 '데미안'에서 나오는 싱클레어도 만났고, 파울로 코엘료의 소설 '연금술사'에 나오는 산티아고도 만났다. 알고 보니 모두 '자아의 신화'를 꿈꾸며 성장해 가는 나의 도플갱어들이었다. 내가 태어나 깨닫기 시작했을 때 나의 별은 작고 초라하게 생각되었다. 너무도 어렸기에 숨을 곳을 찾아 도망 다니는 것이 최선이라고 생각했다.
　어쩔 수가 없고 내가 선택한 것이 아니기에 나의 그림자들을 정면으로 마주할 '미움받을 용기'가 없었던 것이다. 이 책 작업을 하면서 많은 용기를 냈다.
　숨을 곳을 찾아 떠난 필리핀 생활, 수녀님과 봉사활동하면서 받은 위로들, 경제적으로 어려움이 많아서 동생한테 도움받은 일, 작은 아이를 잃고 우울

감에 빠져 있던 상실의 시간들, 다양한 취미 활동으로 바쁘게 산 일들, 기쁜 일도 많았지만 아픔과 슬픔의 시간들도 참 많았다.

어쩌면 누군가에게는 '말할 수 없는 비밀'이다. 하지만 난 이 책을 통해서 어딘가에서 살고 있을 나의 '도플갱어'들을 위해서 용기를 냈다. 그리고 희망을 전하고 싶다. 잘 이겨냈다고…

나는 나의 무의식의 세계를 확장시켜 의식의 중심점에 몽이를 생각하며 동화를 만들고 나의 다큐로 연결시켜 사진을 삽입해서 그려 넣었다.

주제에 맞는 그림을 백지에다 원장님이 그려주시면 색칠하며 분석 치유받으며 만들어 낸 작품들이다. 작품을 완성해 놓고도 세상에 드러내기까지 삼년이 넘는 세월이 흘렀다. '내 삶 백지에서 하늘 끝까지'는 제목 그대로 나의 자서전인 셈이다. 내 책이 완성까지 많은 시간들을 기다려 주신 김영옥 원장님께 감사드린다.

'걸리버 여행기'처럼 나의 여행에 초대합니다.

2025년 봄이 오는 길목에서

김 병 임

Prologue

Everything started from a small dot. Just as life begins from a small seed, it was a great fortune for me to learn about 'Kim Young-ok's Mandala.' My unconscious mind, which was first drawn from small internal movements, was expressed as a dot, and those dots gathered to become lines, planes, larger circles, and houses, creating a mandala. The unconscious worlds that I didn't even know about made paths, created spaces, and the lumps of my mind appeared as a dream. I cried and laughed a lot while working.

And I also met Sinclair from Hermann Hesse's novel 'Demian' and Santiago from Paulo Coelho's novel 'The Alchemist'. As it turned out, they were all my doppelgangers who were growing up dreaming of the 'myth of the self'. When I was born and began to realize, my star seemed small and shabby. I was so young that I thought running away to find a place to hide was the best thing to do. I didn't have the 'courage to be hated' to face my shadows head-on because it was inevitable and not something I chose. I gained a lot of courage while working on this book.

Life in the Philippines where I left to find a place to hide, the comfort I received while volunteering with nuns, the help I received from my younger sibling due to financial difficulties, the times of loss when I lost my little child and fell into depression, the times when I was busy with various hobbies, there were many happy times, but there were also many times of pain and sadness.

It may be an 'unspeakable secret' to some.

However, through this book, I gained courage for my 'doppelgangers' who are living somewhere.

And I want to convey hope. I overcame it well...

I expanded my subconscious world, thinking of Mong-i as the center of consciousness, and created a fairy tale, and connected it to my documentary and inserted photos and drew it.

These are works that I created while receiving analysis and healing by coloring the pictures that the director drew on a blank sheet of paper that fit the theme.

More than three years have passed since I completed the work and until I revealed it to the world. As the title suggests, 'My Life from Blank Sheet to Sky' is my autobiography.

I would like to thank Director Kim Young-ok for waiting for so long for my book to be completed.

I invite you to my journey like 'Gulliver's Travels'

At the crossroads of the spring of 2025

Byunglim Kim (Marian)

목 차

꿈꾸는 별 내 삶 백지로부터 하늘 끝까지

프롤로그 Prologue • 02

chater 1 백지로 여는 길 • 09
　　　　　The road to opening with a blank sheet of paper

1) 바라지 않는 빈 마음 An empty mind that does not want to
2) 좋은 것은 좋다고 Good things are good
3) 부담없이 즐길 때 When you enjoy them without burden
4) 백지에서 부자 From blank paper to riches

chapter 2 내 삶 이야기 My life story • 17

1) 소중한 인연 이어갈 때 기쁨 The joy of continuing a precious relationship
2) 관계에서 서로 아낄 때 아름다움
　　Joy when continuing a precious relationship
3) 서로 성숙할 때 보는 밝은 하늘
　　The bright sky we see when we grow together
4) 감동 나눌 때 사는 재미 The fun of living when you share your emotions

chapter 3 희망! 그 길고 긴 날 Hope! That long, long day • 37

1) 웃고 떠들어도 안전한 장소 A safe place to laugh and chat
2) 쿵쿵 뛰어도 괜찮은 날 A day where it's okay to run around
3) 야~ 라고~ 불러도 좋은 사람 A person who is okay to call "Hey~"
4) 손뼉칠 때 열린 하늘 The sky opens when you clap your hands

Contents

Dreaming Star My life from blank sheet to the end of the sky

chapter 4 반쪽 찾던 어느 날 • 55
One day while looking for my other half

1) 끝까지 바라본 자기 The one who watched till the end
2) 여유로 찾아본 자기 Self-discovery through leisure
3) 사랑을 그리는 자기 self drawing love
4) 생각을 전하는 자기 self that conveys thoughts

chapter 5 아직도 못다한 사랑 • 69
Love that is yet to be fulfilled

1) 만나도 만나도 모자라는 시간
   Time that is never enough no matter how many times we meet
2) 열어도 열어도 더 열리는 마음
   The more I open, the more I open
3) 울어도 울어도 웃음이 더 많은 세월
   A time when there is more laughter even when you cry
4) 아무리 좋아도 내 속살과 같을까?
   No matter how good it is, will it only be like my insides?

chapter 6 언제나 내편 – 자유 주제로 전하고 싶은 글 – • 87
Always on my side –A free topic I want to share–

1) 아버지 당신에게 To you, Father
2) 내 손의 고마움 Gratitude for my hands
3) 딸아이에게 가슴으로 전하는 편지
   A letter from the heart to my daughter
4) 농장 일로써 행복 Happiness with farm work

chapter 7 백지로 여는 세상 만다라 • 107
Mandala of the world opened with a blank sheet of paper

1) 욕망 대신 열정의 꽃으로 As a flower of passion instead of desire
2) 질투 대신 사랑의 꽃으로 With flowers of love instead of jealousy
3) 가짜 대신 진실의 꽃으로 Instead of fake with flowers of truth
4) 위기 대신 안정의 꽃으로 Flower of stability instead of crisis

chapter 8 완성되는 영향력 The influence of completion • 121

1) 좋은 이야기로 자기 자랑
　Bragging about yourself with a good story
2) 하고 싶었던 꿈 자랑
　Proud of the dream I wanted to do
3) 뛰고 날고 싶었던 춤 자랑
　A dance that made me want to jump and fly
4) 젊은 시절 사랑 자랑 Boasting of love in youth

부록 Appendix • 135

에필로그 Epilogue • 156

백지로 여는 길
The road to opening with a blank sheet of paper

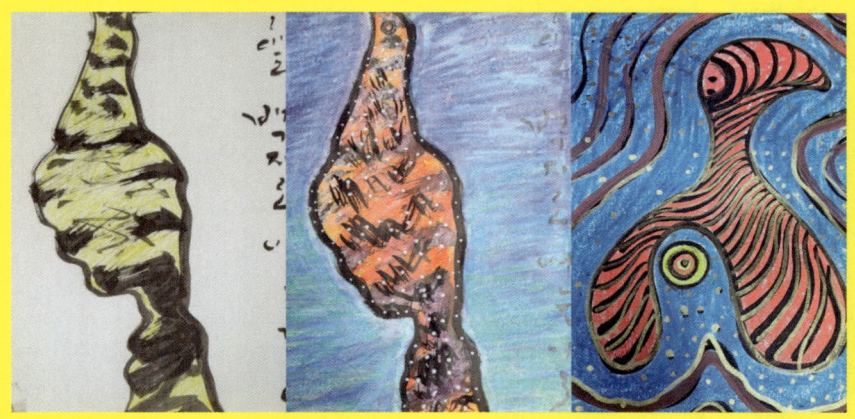

새는 알을 깨고 나온다. 알은 새의 세계이다. 태어나려는 자는 한 세계를 파괴 해야만 한다. 새는 신에게로 날아간다. 그 신의 이름은 아브락삭스이다.
"새는 알에서 나오기 위해 투쟁한다"
- 헤르만 헤세 "데미안" -

The bird struggless out of egg. The egg is the world. Whoever wants to be born, must first destroy a world. The bird flies to God. That God's name is Abraxas.
- Hermann Hesse, "Demian" -

1) 바라지 않는 빈 마음 An empty heart without desire

나는 어디에서 왔을까?
나는 왜 태어나서 마음이 슬퍼질까?'
어렸을 적부터 감수성이 예민한 나는 남들이 무심코 던지는 한 마디의 말에도 상처를 받아 다락방에 올라가서 혼자 울기도 했어.

Where did I come from?
Why was I born with a sad heart?'
I was sensitive since I was young, and I was hurt by a single word that others carelessly threw out, so I went up to the attic and cried alone.

특히나 가장 사랑했던 엄마가 이웃집 아줌마한테
"쟤는 인물도 없고 키도 작아서 누가 데려가려나?"
되뇌이던 말은 상심이 커서 콤플렉스로 작용하기도 했어.

Especially, my mother, whom I loved the most, said to the neighbor, "Jae is not a good person and she is short, so who would take her?" The words I repeated over and over again were so heartbreaking that they became a complex.

시간이 흘러 다락방의 소녀는 책 읽기도 좋아하고 상상력이 풍부해서 늘 삶에 지쳐있는 엄마의 미소를 보기 위해 스스로 위로하는 법을 배워나가기로 했어.

As time passed, the girl in the attic liked to read books and had a rich imagination, so she decided to learn how to comfort herself in order to see her mother's smile, who was always tired of life.

2) 좋은 것은 좋다고 good things are good

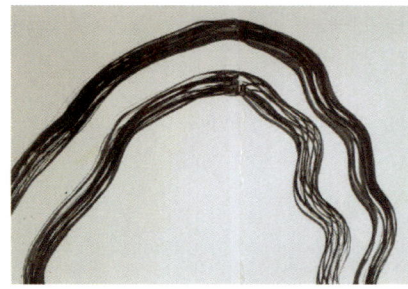

이슬이 모여서 물방울이 되고 물방울이 모여서 비가 되고
비가 모여서 냇물이 되고 냇물이 모여서 강물이 되고
강물이 모여서 바다가 되는 거야

내 안의 이슬은 미운 오리 새끼가 아니야
내 안의 물방울은 헨델과 그레텔도 아니고
내 안의 비는 성냥 팔이 소녀도 아니야
내 안의 냇물은 이상한 나라의 앨리스를 따라가기도 하고
내 안의 강물은 백조의 호수야
내 안의 바다는 인어공주가 노니는 정원이야.

Dew gathers to become water drops, and water drops gather to become rain
Rain gathers to become a stream, and streams gather to become a river
Rivers gather to become the sea

The dew inside me is not the ugly duckling

The water drops inside me are not Hansel and Gretel
The rain inside me is not the little match girl
The stream inside me follows Alice in Wonderland
The river inside me is Swan Lake
The sea inside me is the garden where the Little Mermaid plays.

3) 부담없이 즐길 때
When you have fun without pressure

소녀는 늘 생각했지. '피터팬은 좋겠다'
나쁜 악당을 물리치고 어려움에 처한 이를 도와주고
늙지 않고 영원히 동심 속에 살 수 있어서..

The girl always thought, 'It would be nice to be Peter Pan'
to defeat bad guys, help those in need, and live forever in childhood without growing old.

나도 동심 속에서 늙지 않고 오늘을
소풍 온 것처럼 살았으면 좋겠어.
호수가 보이는 푸른 언덕에서
좋아하는 친구들이랑 신나게 놀고
예쁜 꽃들보며 유쾌하게 살았으면 좋겠어.

I also wish to live today as if I were on a picnic, without growing old in my childhood. I wish to live happily, having fun with my favorite friends on a green hill overlooking a lake, and looking at pretty flowers.

4) 백지에서 부자 From Blank to Rich

소녀는 날마다 꿈을 꾸었어.
심연의 바다 속에서
몽글 몽글 방울들이 올라 오더니
하나 둘 씩 몽이들이 꽃을 피우기 시작했어.
자 똑바로 눈을 뜨고
네가 해야 할 일을 찾아보자.

The girl dreamed every day.
In the abyss of the sea,
Droplets rose up,
And one by one, the dreams began to bloom.
Now, open your eyes and
Let's find out what you have to do.

내 삶 이야기 My life story

다락방의 소녀는 자신만의 방을 만들기 시작해.
창문에 비친 모습을 들여다 보면서
'오늘 보다 나은 내일'을 만들어야지 다짐하기도 해

The girl in the attic starts to make her own room.
She looks at the reflection in the window
and vows to make tomorrow better than today.

1) 소중한 인연 이어갈 때의 기쁨
The joy of continuing a precious relationship

소녀가 자라 어른이 되고 마침내 엄마가 되었을 때,
자신의 딸아이만은
방에서만 갇혀서 꿈꾸지 말고
드넓은 세상으로 나가길 바랐어
드디어 바다 건너 세상에 나가게 된거야
그곳은 말야
일년 내내 따뜻한 곳이야.
커다란 망고나무가 마당에 있고
푸른 잔디밭이 펼쳐진 아담한 집에서 친구들을 기다렸어.

When the girl grew up and became an adult and finally a mother,
she wanted her daughter
to go out into the wide world

not to be locked in her room and dream
but to finally go out into the world across the sea
where it was warm all year round.
In a small house with a big mango tree in the yard
and a green lawn.I waited for my friends

샐리라는 강아지도 입양했어.
시간이 흐르고 강아지였던 샐리도
다섯 마리 강아지의 엄마가 되었어.
새끼 강아지들은 그들을 반겨줄
새 보금자리를 찾아서 입양시켜주고
딸아이도 따뜻한 기운을 받아 성숙해져 갔어.

I also adopted a puppy named Sally.
As time passed, Sally, who was a puppy,
became a mother of five puppies.
The puppies found new homes to welcome them and adopted them.
My daughter also received warm energy and matured.
Sally and her five puppies.

2) 관계에서 서로 아낄 때 아름다움
Joy when continuing a precious relationship

우리집에는 늘 사람들로 부쩍였어
따뜻한 남쪽 나라로 딸아이 친구들이 공부하러 왔거든.
나는 우리집 *도비 요정들과 맛있는 밥을
만들어 주고 주말에는 바비큐 파티를 했어.
이웃집 옆집에 사는 토토킹 아저씨도 친구가 되어 많이 도와 주었어.

My house was always crowded
My daughter's friends came to study in a warm southern country.
I cooked delicious meals for our *Dobby fairies and had a barbecue

*도비 : 해리포터에 나오는 집요정을 비유적인 말
*Dobby : A metaphorical term for the house elf in Harry Potter

party on the weekends.
The Toto King who lived next door also became my friend and helped me a lot.

그 아저씨는 말이야, 음, 처음에는 배가 톡 튀어 나오고
눈도 왕방울만 해서 두꺼비처럼 생겼다고 생각했어.

That old man,
Well, at first I thought he looked like a toad because his belly was bulging and his eyes were big like bells.

하지만 그는 새 키우는 것도 좋아하고
손재주가 뛰어나고 기타를 치며 노래하는 것을 좋아해.

But he also likes raising birds, is good with his hands, and likes to play the guitar and sing.

우리가 바베큐 파티를 한다고 초대를 하면
노랗고 파랗고 빨간 맛있는 칵테일 주스를 만들어 오지.
아! 생각났다.
내 생일에 늘 공부하는 나를 위해 아카시아 나무로
바퀴 달린 멋진 책상을 만들어 주었어.

When we invite you to a barbecue party,
you make delicious cocktail juices in yellow, blue, and red.
Ah! I remembered.
For my birthday, you made me a nice desk on wheels out of acacia wood for me who always studies.

3) 서로 성숙할 때 보는 밝은 하늘
The bright sky we see when we grow together

바다인지 하늘인지 구분이 안 가는 그곳엔
작은 이들이 많았어. 작은 이들은 가진 것이 너무 적어
가난한 자들이야.
그들 중에서도 가장 작은이들을 찾아 다니며
위로를 전하는 엘리사벳 수녀님을 만났어.
그녀는 파란 눈의 수녀님들과 천사의 모후 수녀원에서
사는 데 늘 지프니와 툭툭이를 타고 다녔어.

In that place where you can't tell if it's the sea or the sky,
there were many little people. The little people have so little that
they are poor.
I met Sister Elizabeth, who went around looking for the littlest of

them and giving them comfort.
She lived with the blue-eyed nuns at the Mother of God convent,
and always rode a jeepney and a tuk-tuk.

그녀가 하는 일 중의 하나는 그 가난한 마을에서 하늘나라로
가는 사람들에게 백페소짜리 국화꽃 한 송이 들고
찾아가서 기도를 해주는 일이야.
그녀는 태권도를 가르치는 선생님이기도 해.
아이들은 해맑은 웃음으로 '헬로우 마스터'라고 부르기도 해.

One of the things she does is to go to the poor villages and pray for the people who are going to heaven, carrying a 100-peso chrysanthemum

flower. She is also a Taekwondo teacher. The children call her 'Hello Master' with her bright smile.

그렇게 그녀를 따라서 바닷가 갯벌에 집을 짓고 사는
가난한 이들을 함께 찾아 다녔어.
그곳은 말야,
냄새도 많이 나고 나무판자 여러개를 이어 놓은 다리를
건너가면 따닥따닥 집이 붙어 있는데 열식구가 넘게
사는 집도 있어. 화장실 옆에는 돼지 우리도 있구.
그녀가 우리를 이곳으로 안내한 것은
풍요로운데 빈곤이 있고 빈곤 속에 풍요가 있다는 것을
가르쳐 주고 싶었데.
그들은 서로가 서로를 지켜주며 웃고 있었어.
그러고 보니 그녀는 늘 밝은 하늘이었어.

So I followed her and went to see the poor who built houses on the tidal flats by the sea.
That place,
it smelled a lot, and if you cross a bridge made of several wooden planks,
there are houses that are warmly connected, and there are houses where more than ten people live. There is also a pigsty next to the bathroom.
She led us here because she wanted to teach us
that there is poverty in abundance and abundance in poverty.
They were looking after each other and laughing.
Come to think of it, she was always a bright sky.

INDA Mission - South Baruarte (2010. 11. 24.)

4) 감동 나눌 때 사는 재미
The fun of living when you share your emotions

계란 노른자 닮았네. 생명이 꿈틀거려,
바다에서 저 하늘 끝까지.
겨자씨의 믿음으로 자라나서
멀리 멀리 퍼지는 거야

It looks like an egg yolk. Life is stirring,
From the sea to the end of the sky.
Growing with the faith of a mustard seed,
It spreads far and wide.

엘리사벳 수녀님이랑 우리는 머리를 맞대고 궁리를 했어.
"이 작은 이들을 위해서 우리가 할 수 있는 일은 무엇이 있을까?"
수녀님이 태권도를 가르치는 학교에 가서 우리집 아이들은

거미줄을 걷어내고 청소를 했어. 그리고 교실에 페인트칠도
해주고 분리 수거를 할 수 있도록 쓰레기통도 만들어 주었지.
나는 마음을 함께 하는 사람들을 모아서 장학금도 전달해주고
일주일에 한번은 전교생이 따뜻한 밥을 먹을 수 있도록
밥차 선교를 하는 목사님도 소개해 주었어.

Sister Elizabeth and I put our heads together and thought about it.
"What can we do for these little ones?"
When the nun went to the school where she taught Taekwondo, our children
kicked out the cobwebs and cleaned up. We also painted the classroom
and made trash cans so that we could separate our trash.
I gathered like-minded people and gave them scholarships.
I also introduced a pastor who runs a food truck mission so that all
the students can have a warm meal once a week.

수녀님은 우리를 수녀원에 초대도 해주셨어.
맛있는 저녁도 만들어 주셨어.
우람한 덩치의 파란 눈 벨기에 원장수녀님은
알콜 도수가 높은 레드호스라는 맥주를 좋아하셔서
우리에게도 나누어 주셨어.
수녀원에 놀러왔던
수원에서 온 고등학생들 세 명은
그 작은이들 집에서 일주일이나 함께 지냈어.

The nuns invited us to their convent.

They also cooked us a delicious dinner.
The big, blue-eyed Belgian mother superior
liked a beer called Red Horse, which had a high alcohol content,
and she shared some with us.
Three high school students from Suwon
who came to visit the convent
stayed at the little ones' house for a week.

일로일로 천사의 모후 수녀원에서 (Sisters of Our Lady of the Angels)

그 집에는 초등학교 선생님인 엄마, 미혼모인 큰 딸과
그녀의 딸, 매리언이라도 불리는 대학생 작은 딸,
핸드폰 가게에서 일하는 아들, 초등학교에 다니는 막내딸 니콜,
아들의 벨기에 여자친구 델핀, 거기에 우리 세 명의 친구들.
슬레이트 지붕만 간신히 얹어 있고 이층 바닥에는 합판나무로
되어 있어서 걸어 다니면 삐걱소리가 났어.
나는 그 애들이 너무도 걱정이 되어 삼각 김밥을
싸가지고 자주 찾아 갔어.
그래도 그 집에 가면 뭐가 그리 재미있는 지 서로들 깔깔거리고 늘 웃음
소리가 났어. 함께 밥먹고 뒹굴면서 진짜 진짜 친구가 되어 간거야.

In that house, there was a mother who was an elementary school teacher, an unmarried eldest daughter,
her daughter, a college student named Marion, a son who worked at a cell phone store, an elementary school-aged youngest daughter

Nicole, and his son's Belgian girlfriend Delphine. And our three friends.

The house barely had a slate roof, and the second floor was made of plywood, so it creaked when we walked.

I was so worried about them that I often visited them with triangle kimbap.

But when I went to that house, we always laughed and laughed because we were so funny.

We ate together and rolled around, and we became real, real friends.

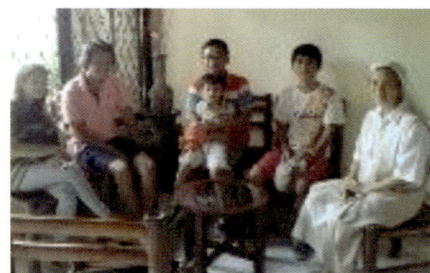 

엔젤 봉사단 (Engel's volunteer) 2013. 10. 29

어느 날 파란 눈의 벨기에 원장수녀님 일행이 아호이 마을로 의료봉사 가는데 아이들을 데리고 따라가게 되었어. 수녀님들은 의사선생님과 간호사이셨어. 그 마을은 병원과 약국이 없어서 주민들이 많이 병들고 아픈 사람이 많았어. 아이들도 건강 검진이 필요했어. 수녀님들은 마을 주민들을 일일이 진찰하고 준비해간 의약품으로 처방해주었어. 도움을 주러 온 다른 분들도 생필품을 전달했어.

One day, the blue-eyed head nun and her group went to Ahoi Village to do medical service, and I took the children with me. The nuns were doctors and nurses. The village had no hospital or pharmacy, so many residents were sick and in pain. The children also needed health checkups. The nuns examined each villager and prescribed medicine they had prepared. Others who came to help also delivered daily necessities.

Ahoy Medical Services (2011. 10. 16.)

  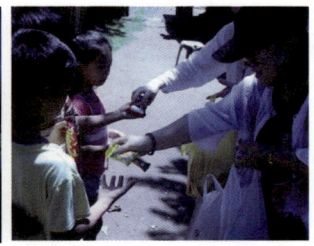

우리는 아이들 학용품과 간식을 준비해서 나누어 주었지.
아호이 마을은 사방이 파아란 바다로 둘러싸이고
야자수 나무와 바나나 나무, 굴이 많은 그림 같은 곳이야.
봉사가 끝나고 우리는 음료수와 굴을 맛있게 먹었어.
물론 파란 눈의 원장수녀님은 빨간 라벨이 붙은 레드홀스
맥주를 굴과 함께 마셨지.
모두가 환하게 웃고 즐거워. 남을 도울 수 있다는 건 보람 있는 일이야.

We prepared and distributed school supplies and snacks for the children.
Ahoy Village is surrounded by blue sea on all sides, and is a picturesque place with many palm trees, banana trees, and oysters.
After the service, we enjoyed drinks and oysters.
Of course, the blue-eyed Mother Superior drank Red Horse beer with the oysters.
Everyone was smiling brightly and having fun, so it was fun and warding.

chapter 3

희망 ! 그 길고 긴 날
Hope! That long, long day

지나가 버린 어린시절 엔
풍선을 타고 날아가는 예쁜 꿈도 꾸었지
- 다섯 손가락의 풍선 노래 중에서… -

In my childhood that has passed
I had a beautiful dream of flying on a balloon
- From the song "Five Fingers' Balloon" -

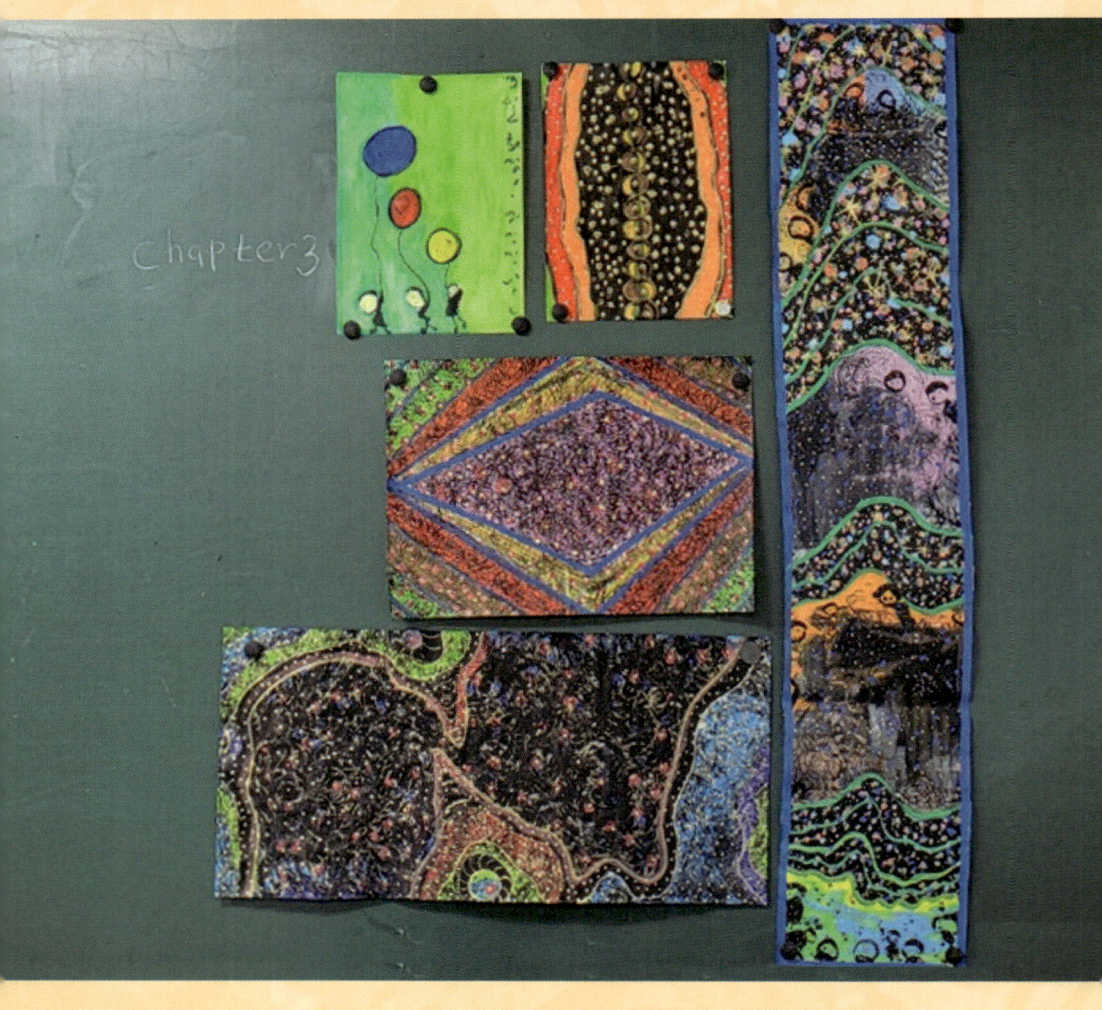

1) 웃고 떠들어도 안전한 장소
A safe place to laugh and chat

'나는 반딧불'
나는 내가 빛나는 별인 줄 알았어요
한 번도 의심한 적 없었죠
몰랐어요 난 내가 벌레라는 것을
그래도 괜찮아 난 눈부시니까
하늘에서 떨어진 별인 줄 알았어요
한 번도 의심한 적 없었죠… (중략)
소원을 들어주는 작은 별
몰랐어요 난 내가 개똥벌레란 것을
그래도 괜찮아 나는 빛날 테니까
(황가람의 '나는 반딧불' 노래 중에서…)

I am a firefly'
I thought I was a shining star

I never doubted it
I didn't know I was a bug
But that's okay, because I'm dazzling
I thought I was a star that fell from the sky
I never doubted it… (omitted)
A little star that grants wishes
I didn't know I was a firefly
But that's okay, because I'll shine
(From Hwang Ga-ram's 'I am a firefly')

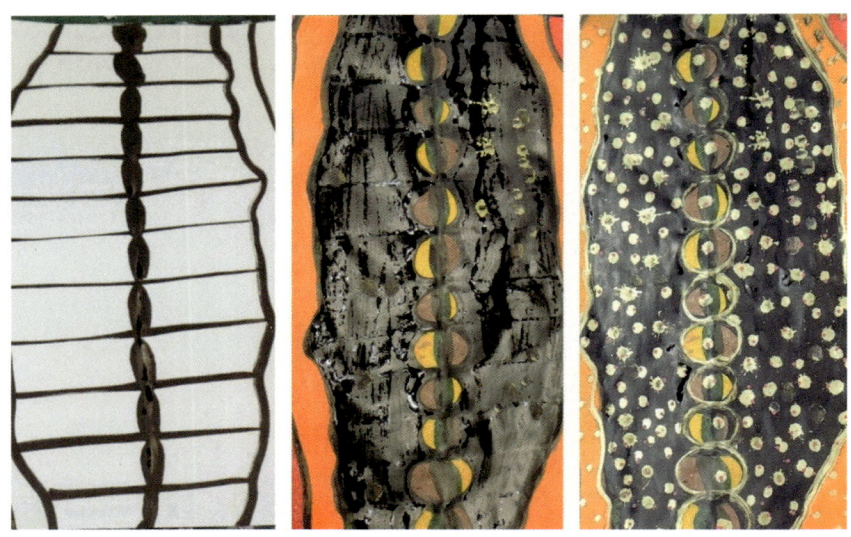

우리집에 온 아이들은 거의 공부하는 것을 싫어해.
대신에 쟁반만한 피자 먹기를 좋아해.
바베큐도 엄청 좋아하지.
바다 수영도 좋아하고

*닥핀 치는 것은 더 좋아해.
싫어하는 것보다 좋아하는 게
많으니까 스스로 행복할 수 있는거야
괜찮아 너 하고 싶은 거 다해.
너는 빛나는 존재니까.
늘 웃고 떠들자! 너희들의 안전한 쉼터가 되어 줄게.

*닥핀 : 필리핀 볼링. 핀을 치고 나면 핀돌이가 핀을 세워줌

The kids who come to my house almost hate studying
Instead, they like to eat pizza the size of a tray
They also really like barbecue
They also like swimming in the ocean
*They like playing Dakpin even more
There are more things that they like than they dislike, so they can be happy on their own
It's okay, do whatever you want
Because you are a shining being
Let's always laugh and chat! I will be your safe shelter.

*Dakpin : Philippine bowling. After you hit the pins, Pindol will set them up.

2012. 2. 3. 레데스코 빌리지, 일로일로 집
튜터 알린과 제이드
2012. 2. 3. Ledesco Village, Iloilo House Tutor Alin and Jade

2) 쿵쿵 뛰어도 괜찮은 날
A day when it's okay to run around

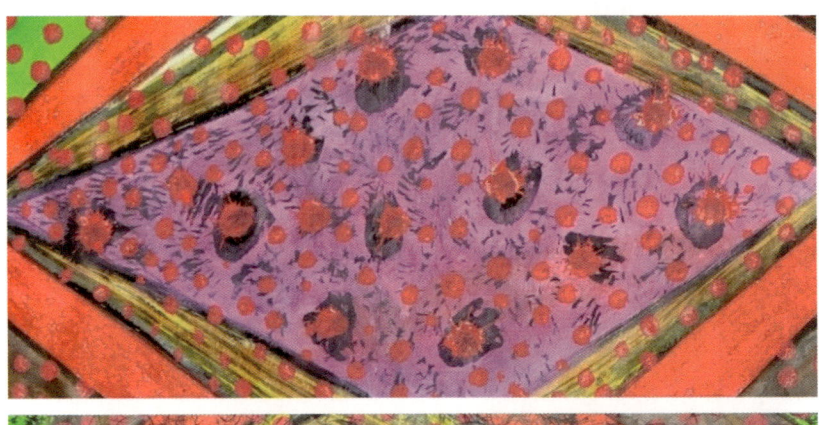

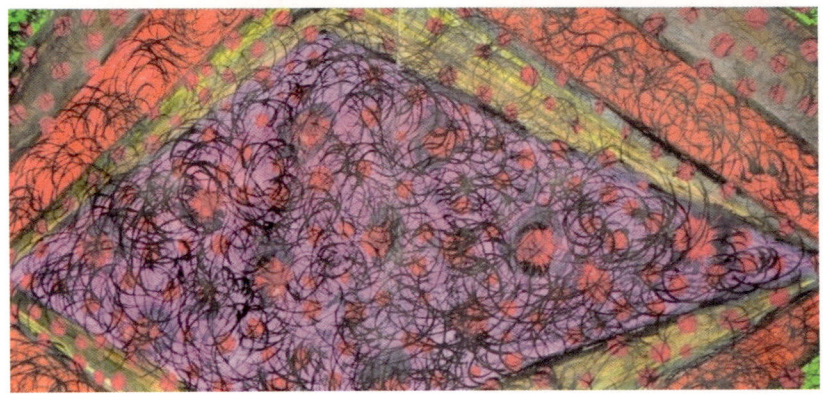

새 신을 신고 뛰어보자 팔짝
머리가 하늘 까지 닿겠네
새 신을 신고 달려보자 획획
단숨에 높은 산도 넘겠네
(동요 새 신 중에서…)

Let's run with new shoes on, bang bang
My head will reach the sky

Let's run with new shoes on, bang bang
I'll climb a high mountain in one breath
(From the nursery rhyme, "New Shoes")

딸아이가 하이스쿨을 마치고 대학에 가면서 이사를 했어.
여기는 십 학년제라 이제 열여덟 살이야.
이사한 곳은 먼저 있던 곳보다 조금 더 큰 곳이야.
말하자면 일로일로 라는 소행성에서 세부라는
대행성으로 땅을 넓혀 온거야.
당연히 샐리도 데리고 왔지.
여기는 앞에는 바다가 보이고 뒤에는 하늘이 닿을 만큼
높은 산과 들판이 보이는 멋진 곳이야
새로운 곳에서 딸아이는 대학교에 다니면서
친구들과도 잘 어울리고 얼굴이 밝아지기 시작했어.

My daughter moved after finishing high school and going to college.
This is a ten-year system, so she's now eighteen.
The place we moved to is a little bigger than where we were before.
So to speak, we expanded our land from an asteroid called Iloilo to a planet called Cebu.
Of course, we brought Sally with us.
This is a wonderful place with the ocean in front and mountains and fields that seem to reach the sky behind.
In the new place, my daughter started going to college,
and she started getting along well with her friends and her face started to brighten up.

사춘기 시절인데 엄마가 친구들에게 더 많이 신경 쓴다고

예민했던 거 같아. 엄마의 그림자를 대물림 해주기 싫어서
머나먼 곳으로 왔는데 마음을 몰라줘서 속상했던 것 같아.
이제는 새 신을 신은 것처럼 자유롭게 쿵쿵 뛰어다니고
많은 씨앗을 뿌려봐! 어제보다 오늘이 괜찮고
오늘보다 내일이 좋은 날이 기다릴거야.

I think I was sensitive during my adolescence because my mom cared more about my friends. I didn't want to inherit my mom's shadow, so I was upset that she didn't understand my feelings when I came to a faraway place. Now, I can run around freely as if I had new shoes on, and sow many seeds! Today is better than yesterday, and tomorrow will be better than today.

2013. 7. 22. San carlos university classmate
딸아이 친구들,
그리고 탑스힐(tops hill of cebu)에서

3) 야~ 라고~ 불러도 좋은 사람
A person who is okay to call "Hey~"

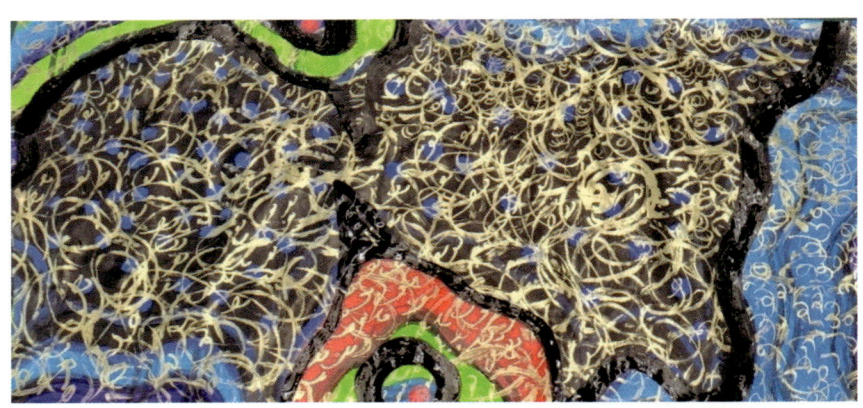

'홍해 바다가 갈라지면 바닥에는
뭐가 보일까?'
바람이 일어나 바다 쪽에서
메추라기가 쌓이네.
(민수기 11;31)

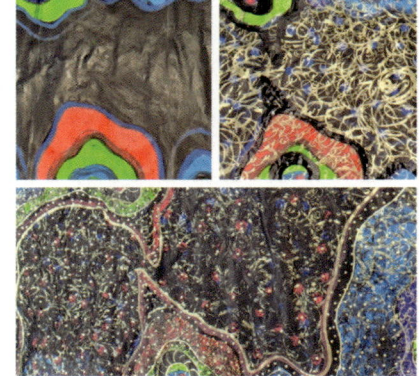

'When the Red Sea splits, what will be seen on the bottom?'
The wind rises and the quail pile up on the sea side
(Numbers 11:31)

우연히 딸아이 유치원 때 친구 엄마를 그 곳에서 만났어.
그녀는 말야, 영화보기, 사진찍기를 좋아하는 화가야.
운전도 잘해서 미지의 세계로 나를 데려다 줘.
아마도 사순절이 시작되던 때 일거야,

신앙심 깊은 힐데가르데 언니가 성당을 순례하자는 제안을 한거야.
우리는 새벽에 삼각김밥 세 개와 커피를 가지고 길을 떠났지.

By chance, I met my daughter's friend's mother there when she was in kindergarten.
She is a painter who likes to watch movies and take pictures.
She is also a good driver, so she takes me to unknown worlds.
It was probably when Lent began,
my devout sister Hildegarde suggested that we go on a pilgrimage to the cathedral.
We set off at dawn with three triangle kimbap and coffee.

구불구불 언덕을 넘어 바다가 보이는 성당에도 가보고
동화에 나오는 핑크 성당도 둘러보고, 사탕수수에 둘러싸여
숨어있는 성당도 가보았어. 그러다가 미사 종소리가
들려 어느 성당에 들어가서 미사를 보았어.
미사가 끝나고 나오는데 까무잡잡한 한 남자가 걸어오는 거야.
외국인 여자 셋이 미사 보는 게 신기해서 그러나?
생각했는데 그 남자는 우리에게 당신 어머니 생신인데
우리를 초대하고 싶다고 했어. 우리는 흔쾌히 함께 갔어.
케이크를 보니 여든 네 번째 맞는 생신이었어.

I went to a cathedral with a view of the ocean over the winding hills,
and I also looked around the pink cathedral from a fairy tale,
and I also went to a hidden cathedral surrounded by sugar canes.
Then I heard the bells ringing for mass,
so I went into a cathedral and watched the mass.
After the mass, I was leaving when a dark-skinned man walked up

to me.
I wondered if it was strange to see three foreign women watching the mass.
But then the man told us that it was his mother's birthday,
and that he wanted to invite us. We happily went along.
When I looked at the cake, I saw that it was her eighty-fourth birthday.

화가 친구가 즉석 사진을 인화해서 선물로 드리고
우리는 배불리 저녁을 얻어먹고 유쾌하게 얘기하고 헤어졌지.
아무런 댓가 없이 순수하게 베풀고 이방인에게 친절의 씨앗을 심어 주셨어.
그들의 아낌없는 순수한 마음에 감동을 받아서 마음 먹었지.
언젠가는 나도 "거기 있을게, 야! 라고
부르면 친절로 대답할 수 있게"

The artist friend developed the instant photo and gave it to me as a gift, and we had a full dinner, chatted happily, and parted ways.
They gave purely without asking for anything in return, and planted seeds of kindness in strangers. I was touched by their generous and pure hearts, and I made up my mind.
Someday, I will be able to answer kindly when someone calls me, saying, "I'll be there, hey!"

2014. 3. 20. 시말라처치 순례길에 (Simala church pilgrimage)

4) 손뼉 칠 때 열린 하늘
The sky opens when you clap your hands

마음에 비친 달 그림자를 걷어 보자.
어린 시절 꿈이 몽글몽글 피어 오르네.
내 안의 마그마 같은 용암이 끓고 있던거야.
첩첩산중 아득한 계곡 너머에도
별이 빛나고 있잖아!
너 그거 아니?
별이 반짝일 수 있는 건

어둠의 시간이 있었다는 걸.

Let's walk away the moon shadow
reflected in my heart.
Childhood dreams are blooming.
The magma inside me was boiling.
Even beyond the distant valleys
in the mountains,
The stars are shining!
Aren't you that one?
The reason stars can twinkle
is because there was a time
of darkness.

나날이 새로운 환경에 익숙해질 무렵에
노동자들을 위한 한국어 강사 제의를 받았어.
그들은 한국어 시험에 합격해야
한국에 가서 일할 수 있거든.
그래서 그들을 위해 매주 금요일 밤에
열 시간 동안 배를 타고
레이테 섬으로가서 수업을 하고
일요일 밤에 다시 돌아와야 해.

As I was getting used to
the new environment day by day,
I got an offer to be a Korean
instructor for the workers.
They had to pass the Korean language test

in order to go to Korea and work.
So, for them,
I had to take a boat
for ten hours every Friday night
to Leyte Island
to teach them
and then come back on Sunday night.

나의 학생들은 물고기 잡는 어부, 주유소에서 일하는 사람,
은행 다니는 직원, 식품점에서 일하는 아가씨, 집 짓는 일을
하는 목수, 코코넛 장사하는 청년도 있었어.
그리고 아이가 넷인 배가 나온 아저씨도 있었지.
한국에서 일하면 고향에서 일하는 것 보다 열 배 이상 벌 수가 있거든.
그들은 꿈을 위해 낮에 일하고 밤에 공부를 해.
나는 내가 가르치는 일을 좋아한다는 걸 새삼 알았어.
학생들이 나를 무척 좋아하고 잘 따랐거든.
종강 할때는 울먹울먹 우는 학생들도 있었어.
시험에 합격했다는 소식을 듣고 손뼉도 쳐주었고
그들의 하늘길도 열리기 시작했어.

My students included fishermen,
gas station workers,
bank employees,
grocery store girls, carpenters,
and coconut sellers.
And there was a father with
four children.
If you work in Korea,

you can earn ten times more than you would in your hometown.
They work during the day
and study at night to pursue their dreams.
I realized that I love teaching.
The students really liked me and followed me well.
When the semester ended, some of them cried.
When they heard that they had passed the exam,
they clapped their hands,
and their paths to heaven began to open.

Korea language class in Leyte University (2015. 7. 26. First batch)

chapter 4

반쪽 찾던 어느날
One day I was looking for my other half

너는 알고 있었어
네가 허가 받은 세계는
세계의 반 밖에 되지 않았다는 것을.
- 헤르만 헷세의 〈데미안〉 중에서

You knew that
the world you were allowed to live in
was only half the world.
- From Hermann Hesse's 〈Demian〉

1) 끝까지 바라본 자기
The one who watched till the end

운명의 수레바퀴 안에서 늘 움직이려고 했어.
나도 모르는 그림자가 가면을 쓰고 잘 보이려고 했지.
때로는 지쳐가고 도망치고 싶던 순간도 많았는데
나를 보고 달려오는 많은 친구들을 생각했지.
그래, '숟가락 속의 기름 두 방울'을 기억하자.
한 방울은 내 안에 집중하고

I always tried to move in the wheel of fate.
A shadow that I didn't even know wore a mask and tried to look good.
There were many times when I got tired and wanted to run away,
but I thought of the many friends who came running to see me.
Yes, let's remember 'two drops of oil in a spoon'.
One drop is focused on me.

다른 한 방울은 주변도 잘 돌아보고
관계를 잘 맺고 좋은 영향을 주는거야.

Another drop is to look around well, build good relationships,
and have a good influence.

2015. 4. 11. Leyte UNV. korean class Teaching

2) 여유로 찾아 본 자기 Self-discovery through leisure

어느 날 숙소에 돌아와보니 내가 가르치는 알란드가 타클로반으로 일하러 간다며 그간 내게 고마웠다며 망고 세 개와 사과 두 개를 놓고 갔어. 착하고 순박했던 그들의 모습에 내 마음에 감동이 찾아 왔어.
노을이 있다는 건 다음 날 다시 해가 떠오르는 것이고
내 마음이 가난해지니 망고 하나에 부자가 되고
내 마음의 중심이 생기니까 주변이 여유가 찾아왔어.

One day, when I returned to my dorm, Aland, who I was teaching, left me three mangoes and two apples, saying that he was going to work in Tacloban and that he was grateful for my help. I was touched by their kind and innocent appearance.
The sunset means that the sun will rise again the next day,
and when my heart became poor, I became rich with one mango,
and when my heart became centered, my surroundings became relaxed.

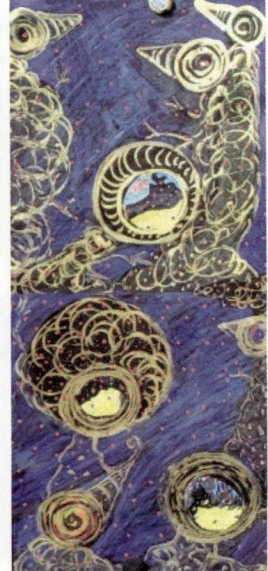

Leyte's sunset

2017. 3. 17.
레이테 키스본 숙소 (kissbone of Leyte stay)

3) 사랑을 그리는 자기 self drawing love

붉은 열정이 타올라 사랑의 씨앗을
퍼뜨리기 시작했어.
닥터 초이와 함께 세부 도청의 주지사님을
만나 한국문화원도 설립하고
소외받은 특별한 이들을 위해 예술제를
만들었지.
팔, 다리가 없고 입으로 그림을 그리는
그레이스가 대상을 탔어.
이 날은 이들이 주인공이야.
이 날이 있기까지 많은 수호천사들이
후원을 했어.
특별한 날 이들을 기쁘게 하게 위해
수화를 연습하고
천사들과 합창을 했어.
돌이켜 생각해보면 정말로 어마어마 한 일이야.

The red passion burned and began to spread the seeds of love.
With Dr. Choi, we met the governor of Cebu and established the Korean Cultural Center and created an art festival for the special people who were marginalized.
Grace, who has no arms or legs and draws with her mouth, won the grand prize. They are the main characters on this day.
Many guardian angels sponsored this day.
To make them happy on this special day, we practiced sign language and sang with the angels.
Looking back, it was truly an incredible thing.

장애인 예술제(2015. 3. 5. KOPEC ; Korea-philippnes Cultural and Education Center)

4) 생각을 전하는 자기 self that conveys thoughts

망망대해 같았던 낯선 별에서 어린 시절 숨어있는 그림자를
걷어내니 용기가 생기고 희망이 보인거야.
돌이켜보니 늘 누군가 나에게 손을 내밀어 주길 기다렸어.
내가 누군가에게 손을 내밀어 보일 용기가 없었던 거야.
내 생각을 누군가에게 전해야 했어.
그러려면 입을 열어야 하는데…
말이 통하지 않으면 생각을 전할 수가 없잖아!
그들의 언어를 배우고 마음을 이해하고
두려움을 떨쳐내고 보다 당당해지는 것.
다시 대학원에 도전했어. 가보자 가는데 까지. 까짓것!

On that unfamiliar star that seemed like a vast ocean, I kicked away the shadows that had been hidden in my childhood, and I gained courage and hope.

Looking back, I always waited for someone to reach out to me.

I didn't have the courage to reach out to someone.

I had to tell someone what I thought.

University San Augustin (Psychological Mastral)
Guidance activity (2010. 4. 10.)
Brgy.Ginomoy Iloilo Leganes high school

To do that, I had to open my mouth…
If I can't communicate, I can't tell them what I think!
Learning their language, understanding their hearts,
Shaking off my fears, and becoming more confident.
I tried graduate school again. Let's go, all the way to the end. What a mess!

아직도 못다한 사랑
Love that is yet to be fulfilled

한쪽 길만 가야할 사람이 되어 한참 서 있었네.
다른 쪽 길을 볼 수 있는데 까지 멀리 바라보며
- 프로스트의 가지 않은 길 중에서 -

Be one traveler,long I stood.
And I looked down one as far as I could.
- The Road Not Taken/Robert Frost -

1) 만나도 만나도 모자라는 시간
Time that is never enough no matter how many times we meet

가방 두 개로 낯선 행성에 불시착해서 미지의 수많은 길을 가보았어.
길 위에서 많은 사람들을 만났지.
찰나의 순간 같은데 벌써 십 여년이 흘렀어.
길 위의 시간들은 반짝 반짝 빛나는 순간들이었어.
열 세살이었던 딸아이는 벌써 스물 아홉 살이야.
잘 자라서 세상 사람들을 하나로 연결시키는 IT 연구원이 됐어.
아직도 난 고개를 기웃거리며 미지의 행성을 찾는 중이야.
나에겐 시간이 더 필요해.

I crash-landed on a strange planet with two bags and traveled countless unknown paths. I met many people on the road.
It felt like a fleeting moment, but more than ten years have already passed.
The time on the road was a sparkling moment.

My daughter, who was thirteen, is already twenty-nine.
She grew up well
and became an IT researcher who connects people around the world.
I'm still tilting my head and searching for unknown planets.
I need more time.

빛나는 순간들(2010. 5. 25.)
Shining moments

1~2)Dream academy classmate((2010. 5. 25)
3~4)With dauther Kindergarden friend in Malapascua Cebu (2017. 5. 21.)
6)Azusa&tomomi Japan friend in my home(2016. 3. 3.)

2) 열어도 열어도 더 열리는 마음
The more I open, the more I open

문고리를 잡고 열어봐!
어, 나의 도플갱어가 숨어 있어.
나의 숨어 있는 몽이를 발견한 건
고향에 돌아와서 은사님을 따라
어느 성당에서 마그마를 만난 순간 부터야!
마그마는 '마음 그림 마당' 이라는 뜻이야.

Grab the doorknob and open it!
Oh, my doppelganger is hiding.
I discovered my hidden Mongi

when I returned home and followed my teacher
and met Magma at a cathedral!
Magma means 'the yard of the mind'.

무의식적인 마음의 응어리를 마음대로 색칠하면서
녹여내는 만다라야. 우리는 그걸 마그마 힐링이라고 불러.
열어도 열어도 응어리는 계속해서 나오는 거야!
마치 빙산의 일각처럼 상처가 빼꼼하고 문을 열고 나오다가
먹물로 덮어 버릴 때 치유가 되면서 새로운 몽이를 탄생하는 거야.
때로 마음의 상처는 훈장처럼 흉터를 남기기도 해.
몽이는 우리의 꿈을 여러 가지 형태로 바꾸어 나타내기도 해.
태고적 원형을 나타내기도 하고 까마귀 모양을 한 삼족오
비슷하게 날아다니기도 해.

It's a mandala that melts the unconscious lumps of the mind by coloring them as you like. We call it magma healing.
No matter how much you open it, the lumps keep coming out!
Just like the tip of an iceberg, the wounds are peeking out and opening the door,
And when you cover it with ink, it heals and a new dream is born.
Sometimes, the wounds of the mind leave scars like a medal.
Dreams change into various forms and express our dreams.
Sometimes they represent the original form, and others fly like a crow, a three-legged crow.

이렇게 검게 표현하는 무의식과 색칠로 표현하는 의식을
통합시켜 상처를 치료하기도 하고 예술로 나타내는 거야!
이걸 탄생시킨 옥원장을 만났어!

음, 그녀는 말야! 돌을 옥으로 만드는 재주를 가졌어.
실은 그래서 내가 그렇게 불러.
가끔은 어두운 광맥에서 금을 캐기도 하고 송신탑을 세워서
우주선까지 쏘아 올리게 만들지. 말하자면 조력자야!
그녀가 만드는 법은 간단해!. 점을 찍어서 선으로 만들고 선을 이어서 면을
만들어 정신의 건축물을 세울 수 있게 도와주지.
그런 다음에 우리가 색칠해 오면 하얀색 마카로 호르몬을 찍어주고 빨간색
마카로 수혈을 넣듯이 찍어 주는 거야!

This is how you integrate the unconscious expressed in black and the conscious expressed in color,
and heal wounds and express them as art!
I met the director Ok who created this!
Well, she is! She has the talent to turn stones into jade.
Actually, that's why I call her that.
Sometimes she digs for gold in dark veins, and builds transmission towers
and launches spaceships. She's a helper, so to speak!
The way she makes things is simple! She helps you build mental structures by drawing dots to make lines, and connecting the lines to make planes.
Then, when we color them, she gives us hormones with white markers and blood transfusions with red markers!

그녀의 제자는 수녀님들이 많아. 어느날 수녀님이 운영하시는
유치원에 참관 수업을 갔는데 옥원장은 수녀님들이 색칠한 그림 중
하나를 보고 누가 색칠 했는지 모르지만
이 분은 목 부분이 막혀 있어 갑상선을 조심하라고 했는데

정말로 그 수녀님은 갑상선치료를 받고 있다고 해서
우리는 깜짝 놀랐어. 우리가 마음을 계속해서 열다 보면
세상은 둥그니까 온 세상 사람들이 다 만날 수 있지 않을까?

Many of her students are nuns.
One day, I went to a kindergarten run by a nun for a class.
I saw one of the pictures the nuns had colored,
but I don't know who colored it.
This person had a blocked throat,
so I told them to be careful of their thyroid.
We were surprised when they said
that the nun was really receiving thyroid treatment.
If we keep opening our hearts, the world is round,
so won't we be able to meet people from all over the world?

마그마 힐링 M 분석가 수료증을 받고(2021. 9. 21.)
김영옥 원장님 작품들과

3) 울어도 울어도 웃음이 많은 세월
A time when there is more laughter even when you cry

별들이 소근대는 홍콩의 밤거리
나는야 꿈을 꾸며 꽃파는 아가씨
그 꽃만 사가시면 그리운 영란꽃(중략)
오늘도 꿈을 꾸는 홍콩 아가씨
나는야 꿈을 꾸며 꽃파는 아가씨
- 홍콩 아가씨 금사향의 노래 중에서 -

Hong Kong's night streets where stars whisper

I am a flower girl who dreams

If you buy just that flower, I will miss the orchid (omitted)

Hong Kong girl who dreams today too

I am a flower girl who dreams

- From the song of Hong Kong girl Jin Sa-hyang -

옥원장은 색칠해 온 내 그림을 보며
감정의 무게에 갇힌 한계가 있어서
열매를 따지 못하고 있다고 했어.
나는 색칠하면서 나의 무의식 뒷마당에서
감춰져 있고
꺼내기엔 가슴 시린 이야기가 떠올랐어.
생각만 하면 울어도 울어도 멈출수가 없어.
나의 작은 아이 이야기야!

The director of Okwon gave me this painting
and said that I have limitations
because I am trapped by the weight of my
emotions, and I cannot pick the fruit.
As I was coloring, a story that was hidden
in the backyard of my subconscious
and heartbreaking to bring out came to mind.
I can't stop crying even if I think about it.
It's the story of my little child!

그녀는 태어나서도 우유 80미리를 넘기지 못 할 정도로
무척 예민했어. 백일이 되기도 전에 감기에 걸려
기침을 심하게 해서 토하기를 반복하고 거의 삼일에 한번 병원에
출근할 정도로 돌 때까지 그렇게 컸어.
돌 잔치를 해주었는데 그 날 엄청 운 생각이 나네.
걸음마도 15개월이 넘어서 하고 그렇게 야리 야리 하게 크면서
언니와 함께 어린이집도 함께 다녔지.
당시에 남편은 중국에 사업을 투자했는데 상황이 안 좋아서
중국에 가 있는 날이 많았고

She was so sensitive that she couldn't drink more than 80ml of milk even after she was born. She caught a cold before she was 100 days old, and she had a bad cough and kept vomiting, and she went to the hospital almost every three days until she was 100. I remember her crying so much when we held her first birthday party. She started walking after 15 months, and she grew up so well that she went to daycare with her older sister. At that time, my husband invested in a business in China, but the situation wasn't good, so he was in China a lot.

나는 아버지 건물이 비어 있어서 고향에서 학원을 하려고
내려왔어. 내가 일하는 동안에 어린이집에 갔다가 집으로 가면
옆집이모가 밥 먹이고 잘 돌보아 주었어.
작은 아이가 여섯 살이 되기 전에 언니한테 한글을 배워서
이 메일로 매일 간단히 편지를 쓸 정도로 아주 똑똑했어.
"엄마 언제 와? 올 때 맛있는 거 사와!
엄마, 하늘 땅땅 만큼 사랑해"

I came down from my hometown to go to school because my father's building was empty. While I was working, I went to the daycare and when I got home, the aunt next door fed me and took good care of me. Before my little one turned six, he learned Korean from his older sister, and he was so smart that he would write simple letters to me by email every day.
"When will you be home, Mom? Bring me something delicious when you come!
Mom, I love you as much as the sky and the earth."

다만 잘 걷지를 못하니까 언니가 롤러 스케이트를 타는 것을
아주 부러워 했어. 늘 그림 그리는 것을 좋아해서 보라색 옷을 입은 자기를
그리고 롤러 스케이트 타는 모습을 커다랗게 그렸어. 또 미키 마우스를 좋아
해서 미키가 있는 모자와 옷을 입겠다고 고집 부렸지.

However, since I couldn't walk well, I was very jealous of my sister's roller skating. I always liked to draw, so I drew myself in purple and drew a big picture of myself roller skating. I also liked Mickey Mouse, so I insisted on wearing a hat and clothes with Mickey on them.

어느날 본사에 교육이 있어서 며칠 동안 시댁에 아이들이 있었는데 할머니가 작은 아이에게 '홍콩아가씨' 노래를 가르쳐 준거야! 그때부터 작은 아이는 홍콩아가씨 노래를 기분 좋을 때 마다 불렀어.

One day, there was a training session at the headquarters, so the children were at the in-laws' house for a few days, and the grandmother taught the little one the song 'Hong Kong Girl'! From then on, the little one sang the song 'Hong Kong Girl' whenever he felt good.

"별들이 소근대는 홍콩의 밤거리~"
다만 여전히 감기를 달고 살고
잘 걷지를 못해서 남편과 함께 서울의 큰 병원에 갔었지.
근데 거기서 청천벽락 같은 소리를 들었어
'근육병' 진단이 나와서 점차 진행이 되면 십년을 넘기기 어렵다고.
우리는 엄청 울었어. 마음의 각오는 했지만 실제로 그 일이
일어나리라고는 상상도 못했거든.
여덟살이 되어 학교에도 입학했는데 학교에서 연락이 왔어.

기운이 너무 없어서 데리고 가라고. 그리고 그 날
집에 와서 잠을 자더니 밤에 배고프다고 해서 밥을 먹고
또 졸리다고 해서 침대에 뉘였는데 갑자기 작은 아이가

"The night streets of Hong Kong where stars whisper~"
However, I still had a cold and couldn't walk well, so I went to a large hospital in Seoul with my husband.
But there, I heard a shocking news.
I was diagnosed with 'muscle disease'
and if it progressed, it would be difficult to live more than ten years.
We cried a lot. I was prepared, but I never imagined that it would actually happen.
When I turned eight, I started school, but the school contacted me.
They told me to take him because he was so tired.
And that day
I came home and slept, and then at night, I said I was hungry, so I ate and then I said I was sleepy, so I put him to bed, and all of a sudden, the little one

"엄마 저기 뭐가 있어" 그렇게 말하더니 잠이 들었어.
난 밤새 간호하면서 옆을 지켰는데 아침에 이상한거야.
마침 남편이 있어서 아무래도 응급실에 가야 할 것 같다고.
그렇게 병원에 가서 3일동안 혼수상태에 있다가
하늘나라의 별이 되었어.

"Mom, what's over there?" she said and then fell asleep.
I stayed by her side all night nursing her, but something strange happened in the morning.

Since my husband was there, I thought I should go to the emergency room.
So she went to the hospital and was in a coma for three days, and then she became a star in heaven.

병원에 있는 동안 작은 아이의 짝꿍 남자아이가 찾아 왔었어. 작은 아이가 그림을 많이 그려줘서 고마웠다고. 작은 아이가 우리 곁을 떠난 것은 3월 26일이었어. 딸아이 생일도 그날이었어. 그리고 운명의 장난처럼 남편의 음력 생일도 3월 26일야 ~
난 작은 아이를 가슴에 묻고 기억하려고 어느 책에 기고를 했는데 딸아이가 서럽게 우는거야! 학교 친구들이 엄마가 글을 써서 동생 죽은 소식을 알았다고. 엄마인 나보다 더 상처가 됐을 딸아이 심정을 몰랐던거야!

While I was in the hospital, my little girl's friend, a boy, came to visit me. He said he was grateful that my little girl had drawn so many pictures. My little girl left us on March 26th. My daughter's birthday was also that day. And as fate would have it, my husband's lunar birthday is also March 26th~
I wrote a book to remember my little girl and bury her in my heart, but my daughter cried so sadly! My school friends said they found out about my little sister's death because their mom wrote a story. I didn't know my daughter's feelings, which must have been more hurt than me, her mother!

그렇게 울음이 각인이 되어 우울한 나날을 보내다가 더 상처받은 딸아이를 위해 마음을 바꾸었어. 눈물 한방울을 웃음 한 숟가락으로. 그 후로 작은 아이 이야기는 아무한테도 말 안했어.
매일 밤 수 많은 별들은 서로 영혼을 속삭이며 반짝반짝 웃고 있어.

하늘 나라에도 악인이 많아 순수한 영혼의 천사가 필요하니까
일찍 데려 갔나봐! 언제가는 웃으며 나의 작은별을 만나러 갈게.
기다려 줘!

So I spent my days depressed with my crying imprinted on me, but I changed my mind for my daughter who was hurt more. I turned a tear into a spoonful of laughter. After that, I didn't tell anyone about my little girl.
Every night, countless stars whisper their souls to each other and twinkle
smiling. There are many wicked people in heaven, so they need angels with pure souls, so I guess I took them away early! Someday, I will go and meet my little star with a smile. Wait for me!

1999년 작은 아이 돌 날에

4) 아무리 좋아도 내 속살만 같을까?
No matter how good it is, will it only be like my insides?

목이 길어 모딜리아니의 여인이 생각 나.
잔다르크의 갑옷을 입은 것 같기도 하고.
아냐, 부드러운 속살이 보여. 난 마음을 읽어 주는 여자야!.

The long neck reminds me of Modigliani's woman.
It also looks like she's wearing Joan of Arc's armor.
No, I can see her soft flesh. I'm a woman who can read minds!

옥원장은 내 얘기를 듣고 여인을 그려 주었어.
색칠하면서 생각했어. 나의 부드러운 속살은 무엇일까?
맞다! 나는 마음의 온도를 올려주는 따뜻한 공감 능력을 가졌어.
난 파도에 휩쓸린 난파선 속에서도 살아남은 여자야!
마주 앉은 그림자를 대면하고 용기를 냈더니 낯선 이방인하고도
금새 친구가 됐어. 잘했어 나의 속살아!

The director Ok drew a woman after listening to my story.
I thought while coloring it. What is my soft inside?
That's right! I have a warm empathy ability that raises the temperature of the heart.I am a woman who survived a shipwreck swept by the waves!
I faced the shadow sitting across from me,
and when I mustered up my courage, I quickly became friends with a stranger. Good job,my inside!

chapter 6

언제나 내편
-자유 주제로 전하고 싶은 글-
Always on my side
-A free topic I want to share-

난 언제나 네 편이야
내 앞에 있는 세상에 하나뿐인 편이야
- 키다리 아재 '밤삼킨 별하나 중에서 -

I'm always on your side
You're the only one in the world in front of me
- Tall Daddy's 'One Star That Swallowed the Night' -

1) 아버지 당신에게 To you, Father

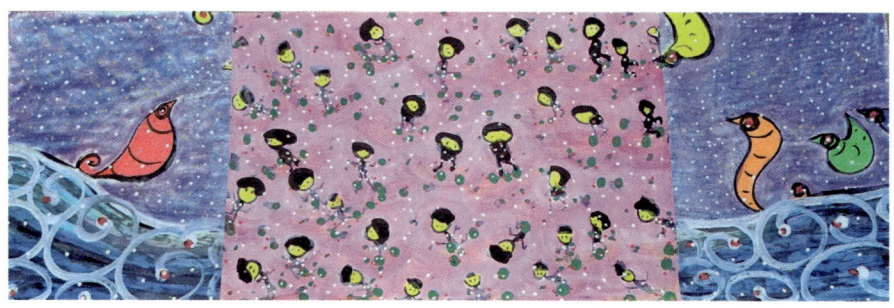

육십이 다 되어 가는데도 난 항상 버릇이 되어 "아빠"라고 불러.
내가 부르면 아빠는 언제 어디서든지 곧 바로 달려 오지.
어렸을 때 난 정말로 유치원이 가고 싶었어
왜냐하면 읍내
사는 친구들은 모두 소화 유치원에 다녔거든.
심지어 우리 사남매 중에 나만 유치원을 안 다녔어.
가족 앨범을 보면 신경질이 났어.
우리 형제들 유치원 사진이 모두 거기에 있는데 나만 없었거든.
난 어려서부터 책을 좋아해서 산타할아버지가 하는일을 알고 있었거든.
산타할아버지한테 선물 받는 오빠를 너무도 부러워 했었어.

Even though I'm almost sixty, I always call you "Dad" out of habit.
When I call, Dad comes running right away, no matter where or when.
When I was little, I really wanted to go to kindergarten because all
my friends who lived in town went to Sohwa Kindergarten. Even worse,
I was the only one of the four of us who didn't go to kindergarten.
When I looked at the family album,
I got nervous. All my brothers' kindergarten photos were there, but
mine weren't. I liked books since I was little, so I knew what Santa

Claus did. I was so jealous of my older brother who got presents from Santa Claus.

그래서 심통나서 혼자 다락방에 올라가 울고 그랬어.
아빠는 자식들이 많아서 별나다 생각했겠지.
초등학교 다닐 때는 아빠가 양복점을 하셨어. 덕분에 엄마가
교실 커튼도 만들어 주고 받아쓰기 시험지도 매번 들려 보냈어.
그리고 선생님들도 우리집에 와서 양복을 맞추었어.
시간이 흘러 어른이 되고 초등학교 동창 모임에 갔는데
그때 담임 선생님이 그랬어.
"너네 아버지가 체육복을 만들어 주셔서 잘 입었다"
순간 주마등처럼 스쳐가는 일들이 많이 있었어.

So I was so upset that I went up to the attic alone and cried. My dad must have thought I was strange because I had so many children.
When I was in elementary school, my dad owned a tailor shop. Thanks to that, my mom
made curtains for the classroom and sent me dictation test papers every time. And the teachers came to my house to get their suits made.
As time passed and I became an adult, I went to a reunion with my elementary school classmates, and my homeroom teacher said, "Your dad made your gym uniforms, so you look good in them." There were many things that flashed through my mind like a revolving lantern.

나는 키가 작아서 6년 내내 맨 앞줄에 앉아서 아이들한테
'꼬마'라고 놀림 받았는데 담임 선생님은 날 '선도 부장'으로 임명하셨어.
덕분에 기 안 죽고 공부도 잘 하고 학교 생활도 재미있게 했어.

그리고 그 당시에 양복점 식구들이랑 성구미 바닷가에 놀러 가서 망둥이 낚시 한 것도 기억나!
어른이 되어 결혼을 하고 자식을 낳아 보니 아빠는 참으로 대단한 사람이야! 당신은

I was short, so I sat in the front row for 6 years and was teased by the kids as a 'little kid', but my homeroom teacher appointed me as a 'leader'. Thanks to that, I studied hard without getting discouraged and had fun at school. And I remember going to the beach in Seonggumi with my tailor shop family and fishing for loach! After growing up, getting married, and having children, I realized that my dad was truly an amazing person! You

'충남당'이라는 빵집, 중화요리 등 할아버지, 할머니는 읍내에서 가게를 하셨어.
동생 다섯하고 6.25때 인천에서 당진 대덕리로 피난와서 먹고 살기 위해 피땀 어린 노력을 하셨어. 항상 부지런하고 일을 많이 하셨지.
할아버지, 할머니는 읍내에서 가게를 하시고 아빠는 농사를 지으며 리어카로 재료 나르는 뒷바라지 많이 하셨다고 들었어.

A bakery called 'Chungnamdang'. Chinese food, etc., my grandfather, grandmother, and five younger siblings fled from Incheon to Dangjin Daedeok-ri during the Korean War and worked hard to make a living. They were always
diligent and worked hard. I heard that my grandfather and grandmother worked in the town and my father farmed and helped out a lot by carrying ingredients on a cart.

바로 밑에 작은 아버지는 그림을 잘 그려서 서울대에 가고
아빠는 장남으로 집안 일 돕다가 기술 배워서 양복점을 차렸다고 들었어.
그렇게 세월이 흘러 아빠는 엄마와 함께 식당, 제과점, 주유소,
차량 운행 등… 할아버지, 할머니 모시고 살면서 자식들 키우고 공부시키랴
새벽부터 밤 늦게 까지 고생 많이 하셨어.
내가 고향에 내려와 학원을 차려서 우리 아이들도
돌봐 주시고 차량 운행까지 해주셔서 항상 고맙게 생각해.

I heard that my uncle, who was good at drawing, went to Seoul National University, and my father, as the eldest son, helped with household chores, learned skills, and opened a tailor shop. As time went by, my father and my mother ran a restaurant, a bakery, a gas station, and drove cars… They worked hard from dawn to late at night, raising their children and educating them while taking care of their grandparents. When I came down to my hometown, I opened a school and took care of my children, and I am always grateful that they drove cars for me.

아직까지도 할아버지,할머니 기일 때 작은 아버지들,작은어머니,
고모 고모부들 모두 모이는 것도 아빠가 건재하고 중심에
있어서 그래. 우리 가족들 모두 사느라고 파란 만장했지만,
인생이 원래 그런거 잖아 !
아빠! 우리 사남매 중에 내가 아빠를 꼭 닮은 거 알지?
키 작고 얼굴이 사각턱인 것까지도.
예전엔 속상하고 울었지만 지금은 멘탈이 강해서
개성으로 자랑하고 다녀.
아빠! 오래도록 건강하고 행복하게 살자구요. 아빠 사랑해요!

Even now, when my grandfather and grandmother's memorial day comes, my uncles, aunts, and uncles all gather because my father is alive and well and in the center. Our family has all had ups and downs, but that's just how life is!

Dad! Do you know that among the four of us, I resemble my father the most?

Even with my short height and square jaw.

I used to get upset and cry, but now I have a strong mentality, so I show off my individuality.

Dad! Let's live a long, healthy, and happy life. I love you, Dad!

1) 양복점 운영하실 때 (1967년~ 가운데 애기 나, 오빠)
2) 할아버지의 중화요리집 개업식 (1972~ 당진 읍내)
3) 할아버지 기일 때 (2020. 8. 17. 갈매못 성지)

2) 내 손의 고마움 Gratitude for my hands

내 손안에 파랑새를 잡아봐. 다치지 않도록 살포시
보라 꿈, 노랑 꿈, 빨간 꿈, 모두 네 친구들이야!

Hold the bluebird in my hands. Be gentle so it doesn't get hurt
Purple dream, Yellow dream, Red dream, They are all your friends!

조그맣고 작은 손으로 부지런히 배우러 다녔어.
나는 호기심과 욕심이 많은 손 이야.
요리하는 것도 좋아하고, 오카리나 부는 것도 좋아하고,
수지침 놓아 주는 것도 좋아하고, 마사지 해 주는 것도 좋아하고,
마그마 그림 그리는 것도 좋아해. 운전하며 여행 다니는 것도 좋아해.
농사짓는 것도 좋아해. 사진 찍는 것도 좋아하고, 글 쓰는 것도 좋아해.
그리고 수학 문제 푸는 것도 좋아해.

I went to study diligently with my small and tiny hands.
I have curious and greedy hands.
I like cooking, I like playing the ocarina,
I like putting on acupuncture needles, I like giving massages,
I like drawing magma pictures, I like traveling by car,
I like farming, I like taking pictures, I like writing,
And I like solving math problems.

내가 배운 손으로 함수에 대응시키기도 해.
쿠키 요리를 만들어서 고아원도 가고
오카리나 연주로 사람들을 즐겁게도 해주고
수지침으로 댕기열도 치료했어.
마사지로 호스피스 봉사도 했고 마그마 그림으로 전시회도 했어.
운전하고 맛있는 거 먹으러 여행도 했어.
농사 지으려고 농장도 사버렸어. 그리고 글을 쓰기 위해 사진을 찍어.

I learned how to match functions with my hands
I made cookies and went to an orphanage
I entertained people by playing the ocarina
I treated dengue fever with acupuncture

I volunteered at a hospice with massage.
I held an exhibition with magma paintings
I drove and traveled to eat delicious food.
I even bought a farm to farm And I took pictures to write.

수학을 가르쳐서 돈을 벌기도 했지.
내 손은 너무나도 바빠 이렇게 손으로 대입해서 미분으로 나누고
적분으로 사랑을 쌓아가니 부자가 됐네.
내 손아! 고맙고 사랑해!

I also made money by teaching math. My hands are so busy
I substituted by hand like this and divided by differentiation
And I built love by integration and became rich.
My hands! Thank you and I love you!

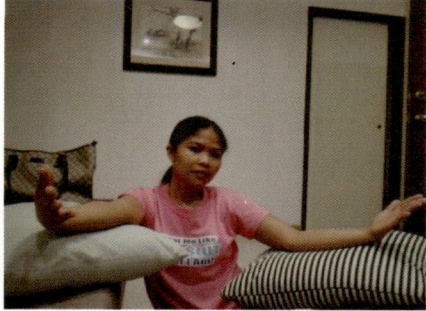

1) 쿠키스토리 동아리 후생원 고아원 봉사(2022. 6. 21.)
2) 수지침 맞는 헬퍼 체체
3) 대전 카톨릭 성모병원 호스피스 봉사(2019. 3. 12.)
4) 대청호 마리 농장 비트 수확(2020. 7. 22.)
5) 농장에 놀러 온 외국 친구들과 감자 수확(2023. 6. 18.)
6) 부소담악팀 대구 여행(2024. 6. 7.)
7) 복수동 성당 성모의 밤 오카리나 연주(2023. 5. 31.)
8) 보성 초등학교 방과후 수업 지도 (2018. 3. 30.)
9) 개인전 '치유의 봄' 전시회 (2021. 3. 27.)

3) 딸아이에게 가슴으로 전하는 편지
A letter from the heart to my daughter

난 잠시 눈을 붙인 줄만 알았는데 벌써 늙어 있었고
넌 항상 어린 아이일 줄만 알았는데 벌써 어른이 다 되었고
난 삶에 대해 아직도 잘 모르기에 너에게 해 줄 말은 없지만
네가 좀 더 행복해지길
원하는 마음에
내 가슴 속을 뒤져 할 말을 찾지 (중략)
- 엄마가 딸에게 (양희은의 노래 중에서)

I thought I had just taken a nap, but you were already old
I thought you were always a child, but you were already an adult

I still don't know much about life, so I have nothing to say to you
But I search my heart for words
In the hope that you will be happier
(omitted)

- A mother to her daughter (from Yang Hee-eun's song)

사랑하는 딸에게
항상 어린 아이인 줄 알았는데 벌써 서른이 다 되어 가는구나!
잘 자라 준 거에 대해 고맙고 미안하기만 하다.
어렸을 적에 엄마가 바빠서 잘 놀아주지 못 한 것도 미안하고
동생이 오래 걷지 못해서 엄마가 안고 다니느라 너를 제대로
안아 주지 못 했어.
너도 아기였는데도 말야.
그때는 왜 몰랐을까? 너의 마음도 아파하고 있었는데..
그래도 할머니는 우선 순위가 너였어.
할머니 댁에 너를 맡겨 놓고 외출했다 돌아오면
할머니는 늘 그러셨지.
"우리 손녀딸 껍데기가 왔네, 알맹이는 잘 먹고 잘 놀았어.
우리 알맹이는 열 아들 안 부럽다"

To my beloved daughter
I always thought you were a little kid, but you're already almost thirty!
I'm grateful and sorry for growing up so well.
I'm sorry that I couldn't play with you when you were little because I was busy.
And my younger sibling couldn't walk for long, so I had to carry you around so I couldn't hold you properly.

Even though you were a baby.
Why didn't I know that back then? Your heart was hurting too..
But Grandma always put you first.
When I left you at Grandma's house and went out,
Grandma would always say,
"Our granddaughter's shell has come, and the kernel ate well and played well.
Our kernel doesn't envy ten sons."

필리핀에서 학교 다닐 때도 학교 가기 싫다고 해서 망고 쉐이크 사준다고 달래서 보내고 망고를 많이 먹어서 입술이 부르트기까지 했지.
또 엄마가 홈스테이 한다고 정작 너한테는 신경을 못 썼어.
그런데도 대학을 잘 졸업하고 캐나다로 워킹 홀리 하면서 동시통역사도 취득하고 IT 개발자로 일도 잘하고 씩씩하게 잘 커줘서 얼마나 대견 한 지 몰라. 게다가 대학원도 잘 다녀주고.
엄마가 학원할 때 SKY학원이었던 거 기억나니?
엄마 제자들이 좋은 데를 많이 가는데 너가 공부 안해서 잔소리를 많이 했어 상처를 줬다면 용서해 주라.

When I was going to school in the Philippines, I told you I didn't want to go to school, so I bought you a mango shake and sent you away, and I ate so many mangoes that my lips were chapped.
Also, my mom didn't pay attention to you because I was doing a homestay.
But you graduated from college, got a simultaneous interpreter while on a working holiday in Canada, and worked well as an IT developer. I can't tell you how proud I am of you. You even went to graduate school.

Do you remember when my mom went to a private academy, it was SKY?Many of my students went to good schools, but you nagged me a lot because I didn't study.
If I hurt you, please forgive me.

그래도 Y대학원을 다니게 되었을 때 엄마가 너무도 기뻐한 거 알지!
엄마들은 다 그래. 너도 결혼해서 딸 낳으면 이해 할 거야.
그리고 엄마보다는 아빠하고 이야기 많이 하는 거 질투하지 않아.
어렸을 때부터 아빠하고 스타크래프트하고
종이접기. 비즈공예 손으로 하는 건
뭐든 지 잘했어. 그래서 지금도 넌 가구 제작을 취미로 하잖아.
넌 나보다 네 아빠를 많이 닮았어.
네가 말하듯이 엄마는 엄마의 아빠를 많이 닮은 거 인정!
공부도 좋지만 이제는 너를 행복하게 해 줄 누군가가 있으면
좋겠다. 항상 밥 잘 챙겨 먹고 우리 행복하자 !
- 너를 사랑하는 엄마가

But you know how happy your mom was when you started going to Y Graduate School!
All moms are like that. You'll understand when you get married and have a daughter.
And I'm not jealous that you talk to your dad more than your mom.
Ever since you were little, you were good at Starcraft,
origami, beadwork, and anything you did with your hands.
That's why you still make furniture as a hobby.
You look more like your dad than me.
As you said, I admit that my mom looks a lot like her dad!
Studying is good, but now I wish you had someone who can make

you happy.
Always eat well and let's be happy!
- Your loving mom

1) 딸과 대만 여행(2017. 5. 11.)
2) 캐나다 퀘백 도깨비 촬영지 문 (2019. 2. 12.)
3) 나이아가라 폭포(2018. 10. 7.)
4) Y 대학교 아카라카 동문 축제(2024. 5. 26.)
5) smart city project (2024. 9. 7. ~ 9. 22)이집트, 스페인, 두바이, 말레이시아, 일본 등에서 학술 세미나

4) 농장 일로써 행복 Happiness with farm work

살어리 살어리랏다
청산에 살어리랏다
멀위랑 다래랑 먹고
청산에 살어리랏다
얄리얄리 얄라셩 얄라리 얄라(중략)
- 청산 별곡 중에서 (고려 가요)

I will live and live
I will live in the green mountains
I will eat water parsley and persimmons
I will live in the green mountains
Yalli yalla yalla yallari yalla (omitted)

- From the song of the green mountains (Goryeo song)

나의 무의식에서는 항상 초록이 나와. 씨를 뿌리고 싹을 틔워서
열매를 맺을 때 몽이들이 나와서 소리를 질러.
살면서 묵혀 왔던 쾌쾌한 분노, 슬픔, 아픔, 불안, 창피, 기쁨, 바람
같은 것들이야. 모두 일하면서 땅에 묻는 꿈을 꾸었어⋯
그러던 어느날 기회가 왔어.
지인에게서 땅을 샀어. 생각지도 않았던 일이야.
지인의 어머니 무덤으로 쓰려고 사 두었던 땅인데
어쩌다 나한테로 넘어 왔어.
앞에는 호수가 보이고 말야, 뒤에는 산이 있어.
배산임수 라고 옛날 사람 말에 의하면 명당이래.
막연히 꿈 속에서 보았던 그 곳이야.
봄에는 말이야 벚꽃이 흐드러지게 피는 곳이야!

In my subconscious, green always comes out. When I sow seeds and sprout, and bear fruit, the monkeys come out and scream.
The refreshing anger, sadness, pain, anxiety, shame, joy, wind that I have kept in my life. I dreamed of burying them all in the ground while working.
Then one day, an opportunity came.
I bought land from an acquaintance. It was something I never thought of.
I had bought the land to use as the grave of my acquaintance's mother, but somehow it came to me.
There is a lake in front, and a mountain behind.
According to the old saying, "Baesanimsu" is a good place.
It was the place I vaguely saw in my dreams.
In spring, it is a place where cherry blossoms bloom in profusion!

그 옆에 벚꽃 길은 지구별에서 가장 긴 오백리 길이야.
난 그곳에 비트를 심었어. 비트는 피를 맑게 하고
장 건강에도 좋아. 봄에 심어서 한 여름에 수확을 했어.
즙을 만들어 필요한 친구들에게도 나누어 주었어.
열심히 일하니까 남편이 작은 농막도 만들어 주었어.

The cherry blossom road next to it is the longest 500-ri road on Earth.
I planted beets there. Beets purify the blood and are good for the health of the intestines. I planted them in the spring and harvested them in the middle of summer.
I made juice and shared it with friends who needed it.
Because I worked hard, my husband built me a small shack.

드디어 나의 꿈이 이루어진거야. 너무도 행복했어
나의 세상이 시작되었어. 야호!
친구들은 대궐 같은 집에 살면서도 초대하기를 어려워 해
내가 좋아하는 그곳은 여섯 평 작은 집이야.
그래도 이십 명은 넉넉히 초대 할 수 있어.
아니 마음이 아픈 친구들은 아무 때나 쉬어가도 좋아
새벽에 가서 일하다 보면 어느새 노을이 지고 있어.
돈 벌려고 농사를 지으려 한다면 벌써 나가 떨어 졌을거야!
어떻게 버티냐고? 친구들이 함께 일하고 씨앗을 갖다 주었어.
친구의 친구들은 주문을 하고 통장에 입금해 주기도 해
주말이면 소풍을 가듯이 도시락을 싸가지고 우리는 그곳에서 모여!

Finally, my dream came true. I was so happy. My world had begun. Yay!
My friends live in a house that is like a palace, but it is hard to invite them.
The place I like is a small house of six pyeong.
But I can easily invite twenty people.
No, my friends who are sad can rest whenever they want.
When I go to work at dawn, the sunset is already setting.
If I tried to farm to make money, I would have already given up!
How did I hold on? My friends worked together and gave me seeds.
My friends' friends placed orders and deposited money into my bank account.
On weekends, we gathered there, packing lunch boxes like we were going on a picnic!

나의 꿈들이 영글어 가면 미술관을 지을거야!

그 날이 멀지 않으리라 믿어.

When my dreams come true, I will build an art museum! I believe that day will not be far away.

마리 농장 (2020. 4. 5.~)
Mari's farm

1) 대청호 벚꽃 길 2) 대청 호수 마중 물 3) 농막 4) 비트 수확
1) Daecheong Lake Cherry Blossom Road 2) Daecheong Lake Welcome Water
3) Farm Shed 4) Beet Harvest

chapter 7

백지로 여는 세상 만다라
Mandala of the world opened with a blank sheet of paper

세상이 내일 끝나도 오늘
사과 나무를 심을 거야
- 스피노자의 명언 중에서 -

Even if the world ends tomorrow,
I'm going to plant an apple tree today.
- Baruch Spinoza -

불루코끼리의 빛으로 가는 길(The road to the light of a blue elephant)

1) 욕망 대신 열정의 꽃으로
As a flower of passion instead of desire

어쩔 줄 모르는 자기 꿈이 많은데 자기 완성으로 가기에는 소심한 것이 눈이 밟혀서 진출을 못하네. 용이 조그만 소녀를 돌보고 있네. 작업해 볼까?
우선 분홍색 집착의 아이를 안정감 있는 초록으로 지워 보자!
열정과 에너지를 한 곳으로 모아봐 자! 그런 다음에 초록점과 흰 점으로 그 다음에 호르몬이 돌도록 붉은 점을 찍어 주자! 이제 자기로부터 역량 있는 열매로 마무리 하자! 와우! 열정이 꽃 피웠네!

There are many dreams of your own that you don't know what to do with, but you are timid when it comes to achieving your own perfection.

Your eyes are trampled and you can't advance. The dragon is taking care of the little girl. Shall we work on it?
First, let's erase the pink obsession child with a stable green!
Let's gather passion and energy in one place.
Okay! Then, with green dots and white dots, and then let's put red dots so that hormones flow! Now, let's finish it with a capable fruit from yourself! Wow! Passion has blossomed!

공부하는 것을 좋아하는 나는 K 교수님을 만났어. 그는 국선도 스승님이야! 대학원에서 선도학을 가르치시지. 미국에서 오랫동안 공부하셔서 외국인 제자들이 많아. 거기서 나는 동.서양의 수련 문화와 심리학에 영향을 미치는 다양한 인류의 정신 문화를 공부했어. 그는 원효 대사와 경허 선사를 좋아 하는데 나는 칼 융을 더 좋아해. 인간의 바다 깊은 곳 무의식과 그림자, 가면, 여성성, 남성성, 개성화와 콤플렉스, 원형 등은 나에게 커다란 영향을 주었어.

I like studying, so I met Professor K. He is a national master! He teaches Zen Buddhism at graduate school. He studied in the US for a long time, so he has many foreign students. There, I studied various spiritual cultures of mankind that influence Eastern and Western training cultures and psychology. He likes Wonhyo and Gyeongheo, but I like Carl Jung more. The depths of the human sea, the unconscious, shadows, masks, femininity, masculinity, individualization, and complexes. Archetypes, etc. had a great influence on me.

클래스 메이트를 만난 건 행운이야. 더불어 그들과 여행을 많이 다녔어.
내 인생에서 열정으로 가득한 나날들이었어.
I was lucky to have met my classmates. I also traveled a lot with them. Those were the days of my life filled with passion.

1) 국선도 승단식(2007.9.14) 포일 선원에서 김현문 교수님과
2) 김현문 교수님, 형님 김현욱 국회의원과 내포가야산 포럼(2008.3.20.)
3) 루마니아 친구 MARCY와(2018.3.3.)
4) 서양 심리학 장세철 교수님과 세부 말라파스쿠아 여행(2020.12.31.)
5) 한서대학교 대학원 건강증진학과 학술대회 발표회 중에(2019.4.)
6) 중국문화 상기숙 교수님과 클래스 메이트 대만 가오슝.컨딩여행 (2019.7.30.)
7) 포일선원에서 수련중인 부부(2008.3)
8) 종교학 민순의 교수님과 화엄사 여행(2018.7.11.)

1) KUKSEONDO ceremony (2007.9.14) With Professor Kim Hyun-moon at the FOIL SEONYEONE
2) Professor Kim Hyun-moon, brother Kim Hyun-wook, National Assemblyman, and Naepo Gayasan Forum (2008.3.20.)
3) With Romanian friend MARCY (2018.3.3.)
4) Trip to Malapascua, Cebu with Western psychology professor Jang Se-cheol (2020.12.31.)
5) During the presentation at the academic conference of the Department of Health Promotion at Hanseo University Graduate School
6) Chinese Culture Professor Sang-Suk Sang and classmates travel to Kaohsiung, Taiwan
7) A couple training at the foil shipyard
8) A trip to Hwaeomsa Temple with Professor Min-sun of Religious Studies

2) 질투 대신 사랑의 꽃으로
With flowers of love instead of jealousy

와! 거대한 파란 코끼리가 나와 버렸어.
감정 정리를 다해 버렸더니 코끼리 코에서 빛을 뿜어 대고 있어.
사람과 사람 사이의 연결이 가짜가 많았어.
남들 잘 하는 거 질투하지 말고 진짜 나의 소리를 내야 해!
코끼리야 ! 코끼리야 ! 너의 파란 물을 즐겨봐!
파란 물에서 맘껏 금 빛을 뿌려봐!
봐 봐 ~ 먹는 것 마다 거대하게 소화를 다 시키고 있어.
먹어도 먹어도 걸리는 게 없네!
너의 눈, 노란 눈동자가 무의식에서 의식으로 사랑도 꽃 피고 있어.
큰 소리 빵 빵 치고 앞으로 나아가 보자 !

Wow! A giant blue elephant has appeared.
After I finished organizing my emotions, the elephant's trunk is emitting light.
There were many fake connections between people.
Don't be jealous of what others are doing well, and speak out your true voice!
Elephant! Elephant! Enjoy your blue water!

Sprinkle gold light to your heart's content in the blue water!
Look ~ You are digesting everything you eat in a huge way.
No matter how much you eat, nothing gets in your way!
Your eyes, your yellow pupils, love is blooming from the unconscious to the conscious.
Let's shout loudly and move forward!

1) 마그마 책쓰기 (2022.3.21.) 2) 마그마 차량 시승식 앞에서(2022.8.1.)
3) 인사동 나들이 (2022.8.2.) 4) 2022년 송년회(2022.12.31.)
1) Magma Book Writing (2022.3.21.) 2) In front of the Magma vehicle test drive (2022.8.1.)
3) Insadong outing (2022.8.2.) 4) 2022 year-end party (2022.12.31.)

3) 가짜 대신 진실의 꽃으로
Instead of fake with flowers of truth

새빨간 거짓말이야! 빨간색 신호등이 보이면 우린 멈추어야 해!
입술이 더러운 자도 있어. 우리 주위에는 위험한 것들이 너무 많아!
무의식 저 편에서 정의감이 몰려오네

There are those with dirty lips. There are too many dangerous things around us!
A sense of justice is coming from the other side of the unconscious

의식으로 노란 경고등을 켜주고 망치로 한 방 먹여주자!
이제 통찰해 볼 시간이야
중심 에너지가 올라오고 두려움을 물리칠 금빛을 둘러주자
방어막이 쳐져 있으니 어둠의 세력은 들어 올 수가 없어.
진실은 영원한 진리야!
아무리 거짓말을 많이 해도 의식과 무의식이 통합되면
쉽게 휘둘리지 않아.
자, 진실의 꽃을 피워 보자

Let's turn on the yellow warning light with consciousness and hit it with a hammer!
Now is the time to see the light
The central energy rises and surrounds us with gold to overcome fear
The dark forces cannot enter because the shield is up.
The truth is the eternal truth!
No matter how many lies you tell, when the consciousness and the unconscious are integrated
You will not be easily swayed.
Now, let's make the flower of truth bloom!

4) 위기 대신 안정의 꽃
Flower of stability instead of crisis

우리는 언제나 위기가 찾아 와!
숨바꼭질 하듯 숨어 있다가
등을 탁 치고 나타나 !
하지만, 마음 근육을 단단히
붙들고 있어 봐!
위기는 기회라고
함께 오는 친구라고 알려주잖아!
고속도로 운전이 무섭다고 했더니
길을 시원하게 내 주었어.
어, 우리 농장이 보이네
호수가 풍성하게 물을 대주고 있어.
이제 안정이 찾아와서 열매만
마음껏 따기만 해!

Crisis always comes to us!
Hide like playing hide and seek
and then suddenly appear with a slap on the back!
But, hold on tight to your heart muscles!
Crisis is an opportunity
and a friend who comes with you!
When I said I was scared of driving on the highway
the road was clear.
Oh, I can see our farm
The lake is giving us plenty of water.

Now that stability has come, just
pick the fruit to your heart's content!

현실에서 도망치다가 아는 사람 만날까봐 두려운 적도 있었어.
그때 내 동생이 비행기 타고 날 찾으러 왔어.
내가 성당은 다닐 것 같아서 모두 찾아 다녔대.
여덟살이나 어려서 마냥 어리게 만 봤었는데..
그로부터 나를 돌보아 주었지.

There was a time when I was afraid that I would run away from reality and meet someone I knew.
At that time, my younger brother came to find me on a plane.
He said that he looked for me because I seemed like I would go to church.
I was eight years younger than him, so I thought I was just a kid..
From then on, he took care of me.

예전에 그는 대학에 떨어지고 분당 우리집에서 재수하며
보낸 적도 있었지. 그리고 전문대에 가고 편입해서 4년제
대학에도 가고 방송 전공을 살려서 알바도 하고 엄마 돌아가시고
방황하다 호주에서 양파 농장에서 일도 했었지. 그리고 돌아와서
SBS 방송국 PD 로 차분히 경력을 쌓다가 서강대 대학원에서
학위도 땄어. 적은 자본금으로 홈쇼핑 회사도 차렸어. 대학교에서
학생들을 가르치는 교수님이기도 해.

In the past, he failed to get into college and spent time at our house in Bundang retaking the exam. Then he went to a junior college, transferred to a 4-year university, and used his broadcasting major to work part-time. After his mother passed away, he wandered around and worked on an onion farm in Australia. Then he came back and worked as a PD at SBS and earned a degree from Sogang University Graduate School. He also started a home shopping company with a small amount of capital. He is also a professor who teaches students at university.

내 동생이지만 잘 생기고 일도 잘하고 감각적이고 사업도 잘했어.
한 동안은 그래도 잘 나갔는데 코로나 팬덤이 지나간 후로
많이 어려워졌어. 동생한테 힘내라고 항상 응원해 그리고 고마워!
"너는 사막에서도 늘 오아시스를 찾은 아이야! 또한 그 물을
가족에게 늘 먼저 나누어 주는 착한 아이야!
너의 깊은 무의식 속의 잠재력을 믿어봐. 네 안에는 열정의 마그마가 있어.
그리고 다시 한번 고속도로를 질주 하자!! 힘들면 휴게소에서 쉬어 가도 괜찮아!

My younger brother, but he's handsome, good at work, sensible, and good at business.
For a while, things were going well, but after the Corona fandom passed,
it became a lot harder. I always cheer for my younger brother and thank you!
"You're a kid who always finds an oasis in the desert! And you're a good kid who always shares that water with your family first!
Believe in the potential deep in your subconscious. There's a magma of passion inside you.
And let's drive on the highway again!! If you're tired, it's okay to take a break at a rest stop!"

가끔은 달팽이처럼 천천히 기어가도 돼. 어깨의 무거운 집을 이제 조금씩 줄여가도 괜찮아. 민달팽이로 집을 비워가도 괜찮아. 너의 중심만 잊지 않으면 돼. 여기까지 달려 오느라 수고가 많았어. 네 안의 행복을 찾아.
나는 너를 믿어.

"My younger brother, but he's handsome, good at work, sensible, and good at business.
For a while, things were going well, but after the Corona fandom passed,
it became a lot harder. I always cheer for my younger brother and thank you!

1) My brother ; META4 Homeshopping production CEO.
2) 세부 에서 Platform K 지사장 할 때 "질경이 마켓팅" (Jil Gyung Yi marketing)
3) 회사 창립5주년 세부 워크샵(2013.7.12.) The 5th anniversary workshops at Cebu
4) 우리 사 남매(My brother and sister)
5) 회사 직원들과 창립 파티 워크샵 (company employees and founding party workshops)

chapter 8

완성되는 영향력
The influence of completion

백년이 되었을 박물관의 묵은 장롱을
The old wardrobe of museum, which must have been 100 years old.
하나씩 열어 에너지를 방출해.
Open it one by one to release energy.
어머니의 태고적 지혜의 신비를 깨달아
Realisze the mystery of mother's ancient wisdom.
주위에 선한 영향력을 퍼뜨려 볼까?
Shall we spread good influence around us?

1) 좋은 이야기로 자기 자랑
Bragging about yourself with a good story

어린왕자 : 아저씨 뭘 하셔요?
주정뱅이 : 술 마시지.
어린왕자 : 왜 술을 마셔요?
주정뱅이 : 잊기 위해 마시지
어린왕자 : 뭘 잊기 위해서죠?
주정뱅이 : 부끄러운 것을 잊기 위해서야.
어린왕자 : 뭐가 그렇게 부끄러우셔요?
주정뱅이 : 술 마시는게 부끄러워.
- 생떽쥐페리의 어린 왕자 중에서 -

Little Prince : What are you doing, mister?
Drunkard : I drink.

Little Prince : Why do you drink?
Drunkard : To forget.
Little Prince : To forget what?
Drunkard : To forget something shameful.
Little Prince : What are you so ashamed of?
Drunkard : I am ashamed to drink.
- From The Little Prince by Saint-Exupéry -

가끔은 말야, 인생이 도돌이표 같다고 생각해.
나의 저 깊은 골짜기 골짜기 마다 DNA 가 이어져 돌고 있거든.
어느 날은 말야, 이 작은 행성 말고 커다랗고 부자 행성에서 태어났으면
어땠을까? 어려운 영어 안 배워도 되고, 하얗고 늘씬하게 태어나면 더 좋지.

Sometimes, I think life is like a whirlwind.
My deep valleys, each valley, DNA is connected and circulating.
One day, I wonder,
What if I were born on a big, rich planet instead of this small planet?
It would be better if I didn't have to learn difficult English, and if I were born white and slim.

혹시 어쩌다가 아프리카 가난한 행성에서 태어났으면
어찌 됐을까? 까맣고 곱슬머리에다 빼빼 말라서 하루 먹을 걸 걱정해야 한
다면? 그리고 어떤 행성에서는 여자는 검은 망토를 머리.몸에 두르고
눈만 드러내고 외출해야 한 대.

But, what if you were born on a poor African planet? What if you had black, curly hair, were skinny, and had to worry about what to eat each day? And on some planets, women had to wear black cloaks around their heads and bodies, and go out with only their eyes exposed.

그래도 이만 하면 행운아지!
Still, if you can do this, you're lucky!

호기심이 많아서 여행도 좋아하고 쿠키도 잘 굽고 책 보는 것도 좋아 공부도 많이 하고 피리도 잘 불고 마그마 색칠도 좋아해. 농사도 잘 짓고 침도 잘 놓고 골프 공치는 것도 좋아해 그리고 친구도 좋아해.
여러 가지 건드리지 말고 하나만 잘 하라구?
그래 좋아한다고 모두 잘 하는 건 아니야!
냅 둬, 난 나 잘 난 맛에 살거야!
머리에 반짝이는 별을 이고 내 열정의 에너지로 하나씩 꿈을 이루어 갈꺼야!
꿈을 이어 갈 때 마다 주위의 환한 빛이 등대 역할을 해 주었거든.
이제는 내 그림자를 걷어 내고 내가 등대가 될거야!

I'm curious, so I like traveling, I'm good at baking cookies, I like reading books, I study a lot, I'm good at playing the flute, I like coloring magma. I'm good at farming, I'm good at making needles, I like hitting golf balls, and I like friends.
Don't mess with many things and just do one thing well?
Just because you like something doesn't mean you're good at it!
Leave me alone, I'm going to live my life as if I'm great!
I'm going to achieve my dreams one by one with the energy of my passion, wearing a twinkling star on my head!
Every time I continued to dream, the bright lights around me acted as lighthouses.
Now I'm going to kick away my shadow and become a lighthouse!

이방인들에게도 빛을 나누어 주고
그림자를 먹물로 잘 묻어 주고
중심을 잡아서 만다라를 만들게 해주지!
난 항상 꿈이 있어서 즐거워

Share the light with strangers
And cover the shadows well with ink
And make the mandala by finding the center!
I am always happy because I have a dream!

2) 하고 싶었던 꿈 자랑
Proud of the dream I wanted to do

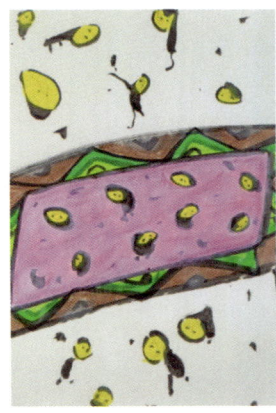 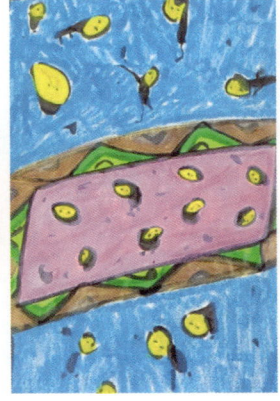 

나의 무의식에는 항상 식탁이 차려져 있어.
남 먹이는 일에 인생을 허비하고 있네, 옥원장이 나에게 말했어.
그래, 난 남을 도와 주는 것을 좋아해. 항상 작은 일을 크게 벌이지.

In my subconscious, the table is always set. I'm wasting my life feeding others, Ok Won-jang told me.
Yes, I like helping others. I always make small things big.

난 축제를 좋아 하는 사람이야. 근데,
바벨탑이 무너져 사람들은 서로 다른 말을 하지.
하지만 난 그들을 이해하고 싶었어. 그들의 말을 배우고 마음을 읽어서
기쁨과 슬픔도 공감하고 싶어 했지.

I am a festival lover. But,
The Tower of Babel collapsed and people spoke different languages.

But I wanted to understand them.
I wanted to learn their language and read their minds,
and sympathize with their joys and sorrows.

예전엔 두려움이 있어서 멀리 가지 못했어.
시냇물에 돌멩이를 던지면 퐁당 소리가 너무 크게 들려.
하지만 바닷물에 돌멩이를 던지면 꿈적도 안하잖아.
동그라미 마음을 가진 사람이 상처를 많이 받았어.
세모들이 너무 찔러 대니까. 네모는 네모 대로 답답해서 알아듣지 못하지.

In the past, I couldn't go far because I was afraid.
If you throw a stone into a stream, the splashing sound is so loud.
But if you throw a stone into the sea, it doesn't move at all.
People with round hearts have been hurt a lot.
Because the triangles poke at them too much.
The squares are so frustrated that they can't understand.

난 바닷물처럼 깊은 무의식이 의식으로 흘러들어 와서
단단해 졌어. 난 인생을 허비한 게 아니야!
나의 꿈들이 열매가 많이 달리기 시작했거든.
열매가 작지만 안에는 실속 있게 가득 차 있거든.
쓰임도 많아서 이제 비싸게 팔아야 돼. 하하 !

I have become strong because my deep unconsciousness, like seawater, has flowed into my consciousness. I have not wasted my life!
My dreams have begun to bear fruit.
The fruit may be small, but it is full of substance inside.
It has many uses, so now I have to sell it at a high price. Haha!

3) 뛰고 날고 싶었던 춤 자랑
A dance that made me want to jump and fly

어머 사다리가 나왔네! 어릴적 놀던 구름 사다리야!
한 손 뛰고 다른 손 뛰다 보니 어느 새 다 왔네!
구름이 우주까지 데려다 주려나 봐! 은하 철도 999 기차가 돼 버렸어
철이와 메텔은 안드로메다에서 다시 만났을까?
난 거울을 들여다 보듯 내면의 내 아이를 보고 있어.
꽃 풍선처럼 날아다니니 춤을 추고 있는 게 보여.
항상 감정은 짝꿍을 이루고 있어.
슬픔이 있으면 기쁨도 있고 절망이 있으면 희망도 있고
어둠이 있으면 빛도 있고 영원함이 이어지면 순간의 소중함을
모를거야! 꽃이 아름다운 건 지는 것을 알기 때문 일거야!
뛰고 날고 춤출 수 있어서 다행이야! 춤을 잘 추는 건 내 자랑이야!

Oh, there's a ladder! It's the cloud ladder I used to play with when I was little!
I jumped with one hand and the other, and before I knew it, I was there!

The clouds must be taking me all the way to space!
It's become the Galaxy Express 999 train
Did Tetsurou and Maetel meet again in Andromeda?
I'm looking into a mirror and seeing my inner child.
It flies like a flower balloon and I see it dancing.
Emotions always make partners.
If there's sadness, there's joy and if there's despair, there's hope
and if there's darkness, there's light and if eternity continues, you
won't know the preciousness of the moment!
The reason flowers are beautiful is because they know they'll fall!
I'm glad I can jump, fly, and dance! I'm proud of myself for dancing well!

4) 젊은 시절 사랑 자랑 Boasting of love in youth

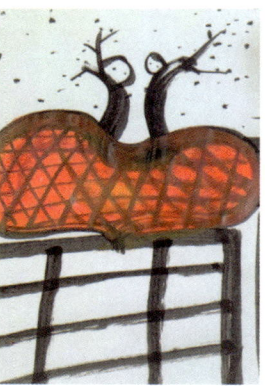

저렇게 많은 별들 중에 별 하나가 나를 내려다 본다.
이렇게 많은 사람 중에 그 별 하나를 쳐다 본다.
밤이 깊을수록 별은 밝음 속에 사라지고 나는 어둠 속에 사라진다.
이렇게 정다운 너 하나 나 하나는 어디서 무엇이 되어 다시 만나랴 (중략)

어디서 무엇이 되어 다시 만나랴
- 유심초 의 노래 중에

Among so many stars, one star looks down at me.
Among so many people, I look at that one star.
As the night deepens, the stars disappear into the brightness
And I disappear into the darkness So affectionate, you and I
Where and what will we become And meet again (omitted)
Where and what will we become And meet again
- from the song of Yusimcho

내가 그를 만난 건 스무 살 가을 정도 되었을 거야!
생물학을 전공했던 나는 실험실에서 병아리 부화과정을 지켜보다
늦어져서 막차를 타려고 버스터미널에서 버스를 기다렸지.
그 날 따라 막차 버스가 30분 기다려도 오질 않는거야.
옆에 학생같아 보이는 남자에게 물어보니 버스가 사고가 나서 못 온다구.
할 수 없이 다른 방향으로 돌아 가는 버스를 함께 탔어.
중간 지점에 내려서 걸어 가든지 택시를 부르든지 해야 했거든.
그래서 내렸는데 나에게 집을 묻더니 같은 방향이라고 오토바이가 있는
친구를 부르더라고. 함께 타자고 해서 겁도 없이 타버린 거야.

I must have met him when I was in my twenties!
I was majoring in biology and was watching the hatching process of chicks in the lab.
I was waiting for the last bus at the bus terminal because it was late.
That day, the last bus didn't come even after waiting for 30 minutes.
I asked a man who looked like a student next to me and he said the bus had an accident and couldn't come.

I had no choice but to get on a bus going in a different direction. I had to get off at the halfway point and either walk or call a taxi. So when I got off, he asked me where I was going and called a friend who had a motorcycle because he was going in the same direction. He asked me to ride with him, so I got on without fear.

그 당시 내가 살던 그 곳은 할아버지, 할머니가 사시던 곳인데
읍내에 아빠가 4층 건물을 짓고 있어서 바닷가 근처 그 마을에서
우리 가족이 함께 살았거든. 그 후로 우연한 만남이 반복되고
버스도 함께 타고 오토바이도 타고 알고 지냈어.
할머니 가게에 와서 장기도 두고 작곡도 하고 제법 글도 잘 쓰고
손재주가 좋아서 무언가 잘 만들었던 거 같애.
군대에 간 그가 거의 매일 편지를 보내왔지. 그렇게 사랑이 시작되었어.
난 대학을 졸업하고 그는 군대도 제대하고 직장을 다니다가
무슨 이유인지 만남과 헤어짐을 반복했지.

At that time, the place where I lived was where my grandparents lived. My father was building a 4-story building in town, so my family lived together in that village near the beach. After that, we met by chance repeatedly,
and we rode buses and motorcycles together and got to know each other. I would come to my grandma's store and play chess, compose songs, and write quite well, and I think I was good at making things because I was good with my hands.
He sent me letters almost every day after he went to the military. That's how our love began.
I graduated from college, he was discharged from the military, and went to work,

but for some reason, we kept meeting and breaking up.

어느날 내 친한 친구가 하는 말이 그를 보더니
"뒷모습이 착한 남자는 바람을 피우지 않아" 어찌됐든 그렇게
집안의 반대를 무릎쓰고 우여곡절 끝에 결국 짝꿍이 되었어.

One day, my close friend said to him, "A man with a nice back doesn't cheat." Anyway, despite the opposition of his family, after many twists and turns, we ended up becoming partners.

호기심 많은 나 때문에 남편은 수 많은 방을 만들어야 했어.
살다보니 어려움도 많아져 주파수가 맞지 않는다며 오랫동안
헤어져 있기도 했지. 그래도 사랑의 열매들이 있어서
아직까지도 단단하게 지탱하고 있어.
그리고 여전히 나는 마음의 방을 만들어 건축을 하고
그는 손재주가 좋아 튼튼한 벽돌로 집을 짓는 건축을 하지.
가만히 생각해보니 우리는 아픔과 아름다운 추억을 공유한
도플 갱어 인 것도 같아!

Because of my curiosity, my husband had to make many rooms.
As we lived, we had many difficulties and we separated for a long time because our frequencies did not match. But because of the fruits of love,
we are still holding on strong.
And I still make rooms in my heart and build them,
and he is good with his hands and builds houses with sturdy bricks.
When I think about it, it seems like we are doppelgangers who have shared pain and beautiful memories!

세상 등대의 빛 (The light of the world's lighthouse)

부록
Appendix

1. 마그마 힐링에서 나의 치유
2. 제1회 개인전 치유의 봄(2021.3)
3. 제2회 개인전 스승과 제자 함께 걷는 마그마의 길(2021)
4. 제3회 개인전 꿈꾸는 별(백지에서 하늘 끝까지 2025.3)
5. 마그마숲에서 나의 발자취

1. 마그마 힐링에서의 나의 치유

마그마 힐링 1급 과정을 할 때였다. 다른 작품에서 도태되어 나온 몽이를 칼로 자르고 다른 도화지에 옮겨 붙였는데 원장님은 그림자가 많다며 먹물로 묻었다.

순간 작은 아이 추억이 떠올라 엄청 눈물을 쏟았다. 점을 찍지 못하고 훌쩍이니 원장님께서 하얀 호르몬과 빨간 호르몬으로 수혈을 해주니 어둠 속에서 노란 유채꽃과 동백꽃이 피어 나기 시작했다. 눈내리는 겨울날에도 동백꽃을 피우는 나의 모습이다. 목에 있는 흉터까지도 나를 닮았다.

〈동백꽃 새〉

워크북을 색칠하다 맘에 안들어 먹물로 덮고 만다라 워크북을 오려서 붙였다. 중심을 잡고 비어 있는 공간에는 분홍색을 칠해줌.

〈분홍 나비의 아리랑〉

비상하는 양쪽 몽이의 눈과 빨강, 하양 호르몬 찍어주니 어린시절 나비를 따라다니던 추억이 연상되어 기분이 좋아짐

　부암동 옥탑방에서 밤새서 작업했던 작품이다. 워크북에 숲속에 나무가 많이 그려져 있었는데 몽이 그림자가 나오질 못하고 있었다. 나의 무의식은 광산에 밤새 벽돌을 그렸다. 날아오르고 싶은데 날지를 못하니 갈비뼈를 드러내고 껍데기를 탈피를 해야 한다 더 높이 더 멀리 친구의 아들이 우울증이 있어서 집 밖으로 안나온다기에 생각하며 마무리했다.

〈도요새의 비밀〉

수레바퀴아래서 길을 찾다

반복되는 일상에서 벗어 나고자 바퀴를 굴리고자 했다. 나의 무의식의 억압은 나도 모르게 밤새 벽돌 작업으로 산을 만들고 있었다. 스스로 방어막을 만들어 바위로 겹겹이 울타리로 막혔는데 바퀴 안에 빨간 중심을 넣어 내적으로 단단해지고 정신의 건축물을 세울 수 있었다.

하얀 호르몬을 주입해서 전체적으로 막혀 있던 부분이 뚫리고 기름칠해서 모든 것이 돌아가고 순환되었다.

2. 제1회 개인전 치유의 봄 (2021.3)

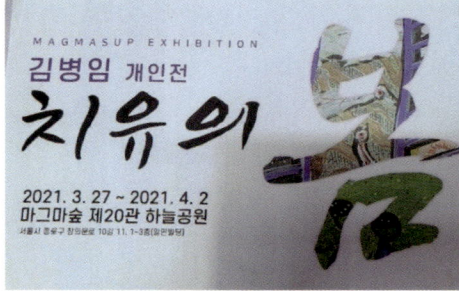

전시회 축하해 주러 온 고등학교 친구 금희, 경선
그리고 대학원 종교학 민순의 교수님, 권대표, 초롱주단 원장님
(2021.3.27.)

〈1회 전시회 작품들〉

가족분들과 친구들,지인들 많은 분들이 참석해 주어 자리가 빛났다. 거의 백 여점의 작품들을 열 단계로 분류하여 테마별로 주제를 나누어 첫 번째 '묵시적 사유'에서 열 번째 '내 마음의 연금 술사'에 이르기까지 분류했다.

〈빛의 만다라〉

3. 제2회 개인전 스승과 제자 함께 걷는 마그마의 길 (2021.9)

고등학교 가정선생님이셨던 은사님을 따라 마그마 숲에 입문하여 함께 전시회를 여는 행운을 얻었다. 함께 작업하는 많은 선생님들이 축하를 해 주었다. 제2회 전시회는 'M 분석 과정'으로 물이 흐르게, 기름이 돌게 하는 통합과정이면서 감정의 찌꺼기를 거르는 "똥 시리즈" 작업을 많이 했다. 특히나 거대한 코끼리 상징물이 나와서 오십여 년 넘게 쌓아온 무의식의 찌꺼기인 변비 작업을 유쾌하게 풀어 내기도 했던 것이 기억에 많이 남았다.

은사님과 대학원 종교학 교수님, 클래스메이트인 초롱주단 원장님

〈제2회 전시회 작품들〉

이 작품을 작업하면서 내 농장에 농막과 비닐 하우스가 있으면 좋겠다고 생각했는데 기적적으로 남편이 작품과 똑같이 만들어 주었다.

4. 제3회 개인전 꿈꾸는 별 (백지에서 하늘 끝까지 2025.3)

5. 마그마 숲에서 나의 발자취

글로벌 리더쉽 워크숍
2020.7.25. 파 출판단지 지혜의 숲

2021. 4. 6. 나산다 다산다 뇌 워크숍 (대전 향수뜰)
우리 농장 (마리 농장)에서 비트 심기 체험

2021.9.14.~ 10.14 '당진 예꿈 아동 지역 센타' (4회기)

아이들은 나라의 미래다. 마그마힐링을 통해 그들의 꿈이 영글어 간다.

2021.7.16.~8.31 공주 가족 지원 센타 (12회기)

공주 이영희 소장님의 소개로 보조강사로 들어 갔다.
수업 받는 선생님들이 너무 진지해서 표현하는 것을 두려워했지만 차츰
표정이 밝아 졌다. 치유자의 다양한 모습을 경험해서 좋았다.

2019.10.9.~ 2020.12 부암동 워크샵

옥원장님의 새로운 책이 출판될 때마다 은사님과 함께 부암동 워크샵에 참여 했다. 워크북 종류는 수 백가지 이상이다. 본인이 원하는 대로 선택할 수 있다.

2021.3~2024. 9 부암동 전시회, 포천 워크샵

마그마와 인연을 맺은지도 벌써 5년이란 세월이 흘렀다.
하나 하나씩 도전하면서 이루어 낸 일들이 꿈만 같기만 하다.
나의 책을 계기로 조금씩 천천히 외국인들도 마그마를 알아갔으면 하는 바램이 있다. 이제 그들에게도 마그마 농사의 씨앗을 뿌릴 것이다.
잘 자라서 민들레 홀씨가 퍼지듯 지구촌 방방곡곡 퍼지길 소망해 본다

- 2025. 2. 김병임 -

에필로그

'내 삶 백지로부터 하늘 끝까지' 아직도 진행 중이다. 뒷마당처럼 감춰져 있고 드러나지 못했던 구석진 곳까지 확장된 삶으로 연결해 보려고 노력했다.

사람들 마다 누구나 감추고 싶은 비밀이 있다. 조그만 흠집이라도 드러냈을 때는 누군가에게는 하늘이 무너지는 슬픔을 경험하고 또 어느 누군가는 남에게 비수같은 말을 던져 놓고도 태연하게 언제 그랬나 싶을 정도로 잊어 버린다. 내면의 상처는 빙산의 일각과 같아서 비슷한 상황이 오면 트라우마를 낳기도 하고 시간이 흐르면 서서히 무뎌지기도 하지만 곪아서 터지거나 폭발하기도 하고 치유 받았다 하더라도 가슴에 흉터는 남기 마련이다. 어른들은 늘 참고 인내하는 것이 미덕이라고 했다.

그러면서 양처럼 순하면 무시당하고 여우처럼 교묘하게 잘살면 오히려 부러움의 대상이라고 말한다. 이처럼 세상과의 관계에서 마음의 희노애락이 내 마음의 감정에 영향을 미칠 때 어떤이는 우울감을 경험하게 된다.

내가 아는 지인의 친구는 우울감이 심해 밖에 나오는 것을 거부하고 사람 만나는 것을 꺼린다고 한다. 모두 마음 근육이 여리기 때문이다. 다행히 난 운이 좋아 마그마 힐링으로 근육이 커지고 있다. 워크북으로 색칠하고 분석 받으면서 길을 내기도 하고 집을 지으면서 내 안의 숨어 있는 만다라를 만났다. 만다라는 나의 무의식과 의식이 만나는 중심에서 여러 가지 모양으로 나타난다. 우리는 그것을 몽이라고 부른다.

몽이의 여행길에서 붕대를 두르고 있는 몽이, 베인 상처를 감추려고 애쓰는 자화상의 몽이도 만났다. 그러다 친구들과 즐겁게 노니는 몽이와 빨간 열매를 마구 마구 따서 우주선 타고 소풍가는 몽이도 만났다. 몽이와 함께 가는 길은 치유의 과정이다. 도피처럼 떠났던 십 여년 외국 생활에서 길 위에서 많은 천사들을 만났다. 가난하지만 마음을 내주고 밝게 집으로 초대해준 따뜻한 친구들도 늘 기억하고 싶어 책에 담았다. 그들에게는 내가 이방인 이었을텐데 친절을 베풀어 준 이들이 많았다. 당시에는 늘 나쁜 기억만 되뇌이고 있었는데 돌이켜 보니 좋은 기억이 더 많았다. 빛나는 순간들이었다.

나는 내 주위에 이방인들을 친구로 맞이할 준비를 하고 있다. 조그만 시작으로 내 책에도 그들의 언어로 기록해 놓았다. 길을 떠나 보자! 친구 찾으러!

"나는 백지에서 하늘 끝 까지 여행하는 꿈 꾸는 별이다"

2025년 3월 봄을 기다리며
김 병 임

Epilogue

'My life from blank sheet to the end of the sky' is still in progress. I tried to connect it to a life that has expanded to the corners that were hidden and undisclosed like a backyard.

Everyone has a secret they want to hide. When even a small flaw is revealed, some people experience the sadness of the sky falling down, and others throw sharp words at others and then forget about it as if it never happened.

The wounds inside are like the tip of the iceberg. When a similar situation occurs, it can cause trauma, and it can gradually become dull over time, but it can also burst or explode, and even if it heals, it leaves a scar on the heart. Adults always say that patience and endurance are virtues. They say that if you are gentle like a sheep, you will be ignored, and if you live cleverly like a fox, you will be envied. In this way, when the joys and sorrows of the heart affect the emotions of my heart in my relationship with the world, some people experience depression.

A friend of mine says that he is depressed and refuses to go out and meets people. It's because his heart muscles are weak. Fortunately, I'm lucky and my muscles are growing thanks to Magma Healing. While coloring and analyzing the workbook, I made a path and built a house, and I met the mandala hidden inside me. The mandala appears in various shapes at the center where my unconscious and conscious meet. We call it Mong.

On Mong's journey, we met Mong wearing a bandage, and Mong in a self-portrait trying to hide his wounds. Then we met Mong playing happily with friends, and Mong picking red berries and going on a picnic on a spaceship. The road we take with Mong is a healing process. During the ten years of living abroad that I left as if I was escaping, I met many angels on the road. I wanted to always remember the warm friends who were poor but opened their hearts and invited me into their homes, so I included them in the book.

To them, I must have been a stranger, but there were many who showed me kindness. At the time, I only had bad memories,
but looking back, there were more good memories. Those were shining moments.
I am preparing to welcome strangers around me as friends. I have written in their language in my book, starting with a small beginning. Let's go on a journey! To find friends!
"I am a star that dreams of traveling from a blank sheet of paper to the ends of the sky."

Waiting for spring in March 2025
Byunglim Kim (Marian)

꿈꾸는 별
내 삶 백지로부터 하늘 끝까지

Dreaming star
My life from blank sheet to the end of the sky

발행일	2025년 3월 1일
지은이	김 병 임
	TEL : 010-5346-5627

펴낸곳	마그마숲
	1~2관(인간탐색관) 5~6관(블랙투시관) : 경기도 포천시 영북면 문암길 24
	3~4관(정신탐색관) : 경기도 포천시 신북면 청신로2084
	7관(생활탐색관) ~8관(몸탐색관) : 경기도 포천시 신북면 기지리 101-6
	9관(관계탐색관) : 대구광역시 수성구 동원로 150(만촌동)
	TEL : 031-533-1707　FAX : 031-532-1706
이메일	magmasup@naver.com
홈페이지	마그마숲 www.magmasup.co.kr
ISBN	979-11-7330-049-3
정가	30,000원

※이 책을 무단 전재 또는 복제 행위 시 저작권법에 따라 처벌 받게 됩니다.